The Q Guide to

Amsterdam

The Q Guides

FROM ALYSON BOOKS

TRAVEL & LEISURE

Q

GUIDE

OUT THERE

The Q Guide to

Amsterdam

**Stuff You Didn't Even Know You Wanted
to Know**...about Europe's most
liberated, notorious city

[dara colwell, m.a.]

alyson books
NEW YORK

THIS TRADE PAPERBACK ORIGINAL IS PUBLISHED BY
ALYSON BOOKS
P.O. BOX 1253
OLD CHELSEA STATION
NEW YORK, NEW YORK 10113-1251

DISTRIBUTION IN THE UNITED KINGDOM BY
TURNAROUND PUBLISHER SERVICES LTD.
UNIT 3, OLYMPIA TRADING ESTATE,
COBURG ROAD, WOOD GREEN,
LONDON N22 6TZ UNITED KINGDOM

FIRST EDITION: FEBRUARY 2007

06 07 08 09 10 [a] 10 9 8 7 6 5 4 3 2 1

ISBN 1-55583-980-0
ISBN-13 978-1-55583-980-2

LIBRARY OF CONGRESS CATALOGING-IN-PUBLICATION
DATA IS ON FILE.

ALL PHOTOGAPHS © DARA COLWELL
COVER PHOTOGRAPH COURTESY VEER
MAP DESIGN BY NIKOLETT GYOZTES

For those gays, especially Dutch gays,
on the forefront for equal rights—
sexual, social, and most importantly, political.

Contents

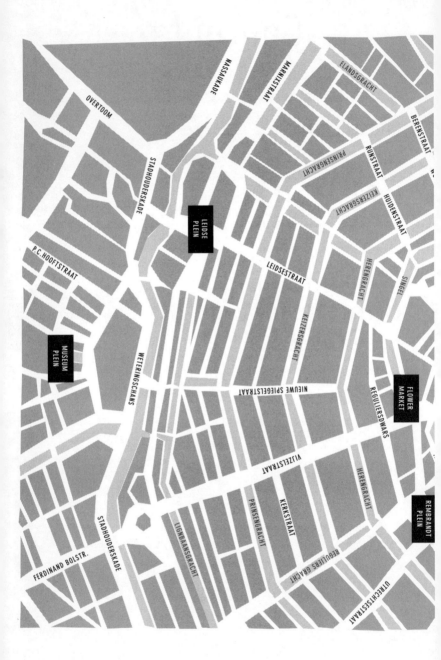

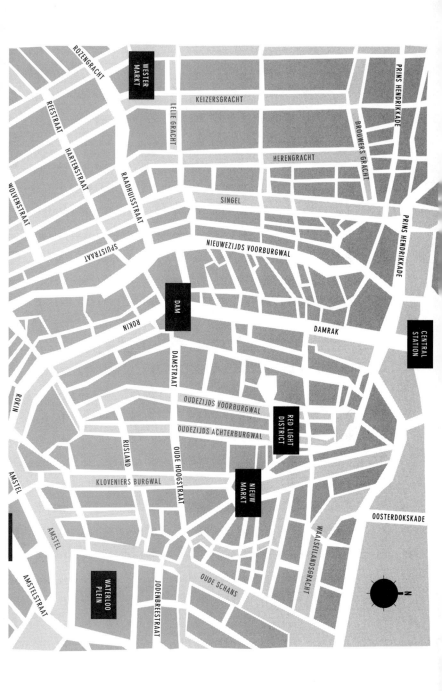

THE AMSTERDAMMERTJE OF ALL TIME:
THE WAR MONUMENT AT DAM SQUARE.

Introduction

Ruled by a queen and surrounded by dykes, Amsterdam is a city where nothing's taboo.

CONSIDERED EUROPE'S first Gay Mecca, this forward-thinking capital was light years ahead of the rest of the world, openly celebrating gay sex when most major cities could only mouth it. While cities such as Paris, Barcelona, London, and Berlin rightfully boast an extravagant gay nightlife, Amsterdam is politically ripe, a gay capital first—never a gay ghetto—where explicit sleaze exists alongside innocent pursuits and diversity is key. Ruled by a queen and surrounded by dykes, Amsterdam is a city where nothing is taboo.

With more than 100 gay bars and venues, this modest-sized metropolis still houses Europe's largest gay scene and there is no shortage of adventure in a city that prides itself on its reputation for sexual license, if not licentiousness. In Amsterdam, size definitely matters. Cosmopolitan yet compact, the city's gay epicenter

10 REASONS TO VISIT AMSTERDAM

1. To experience—even if temporarily—life in the capital of a country with liberal policies.
2. To bike wherever you want, whenever you want, and always have the right of way.
3. To slip into a wide array of darkrooms—what they lack in romance, they make up for in efficiency.
4. No Starbucks.
5. To celebrate Queen's Day, an unregulated street party/flea market where thousands of orange-clad inhabitants traipse through the city like it's carnival (unfortunately, with considerably more clothing).
6. One stop gay shopping—where else can you buy a multi-colored penis, a pair of clogs, a novelty lighter, and tickets to a circuit party all in the same shop?
7. To see semi-naked prostitutes text-messaging from their neon-lit windows deep within the Disneyland of sleaze.
8. To get out of the ghetto—there are gays wherever you go.
9. To see Vondelpark's wild parrots (supposedly the progeny of escaped pets) that squawk freely from the treetops.
10. To smoke weed with a police officer, or whoever it is you pick up at the bar.

makes bar hopping easy and cruising highly accessible. Decades of social integration have created a diverse gay scene ranging from trendy Reguliersdwarsstraat, where bronzed fashionistas drink and flirt, to the Red Light District's gritty Warmoesstraat, crowded with leather boys tugging at each other's chaps.

Never mind the centuries-old windmills, liberal sex and drug laws coupled with forward-thinking ideas have ensured a progressive social landscape no European city can rival. In recent centuries, Amsterdam has offered gays and lesbians greater freedom than almost any city on earth. Homosexuality was decriminalized decades before the Victorians invented underwear; the city opened its first gay bar in 1927; and in 2001, when the country was the world's first to legalize gay marriage, Amsterdam's mayor conducted the first same-sex services.

And there's more. Host to the Gay Games in 1998 and the world's only floating gay pride parade, Amsterdam maintains its rank as a top gay destination—and a popular destination, period. Amsterdam is one of Europe's most scenic cities. A cold, grayish heaven with elegant, narrow canals and stylish streets that boast a beautiful sense of quiet (outside the Red Light District, of course), Amsterdam prides itself as a cosmopolitan village with the savvy and charm to rival major European capitals. Considering this city with 750,000 inhabitants draws more than four million visitors each year, the match is more or less even.

If you gauge gayness by mega clubs and their endless supply of shirtless boys, then Amsterdam doesn't fit the stereotypical bill. Its greatest attraction is more attitude than architecture—the buzz word here is acceptance. Thanks to the Dutch, Amsterdam remains one of the world's most tolerant cities, a true magnet for gay globetrotters and an erotic must-see for those pursuing sexual—not to mention political—freedom.

A SEA OF BIKES, WHICH EASILY OUTNUMBER PIGEONS.

CHAPTER 1

Amsterdam's Gay History

QUOTE

"I'm God's creature and not a caricature."

—Gerard Reve, Famous Dutch poet who came out in his forties, from *Op Weg Naar Het Einde*, 1963

THE DUTCH have a reputation—almost cliché—for being liberal and when it comes to homosexuality, mainstream attitudes in recent decades have remained reasonably tolerant. On the forefront of advancing gay rights, Holland decriminalized homosexuality in 1811; lowered the age of consent for gay men to 16 in 1971; and in 2001, trumped other nations by legalizing same-sex marriage. In the first year alone, 1,300 male and 1,100 female couples wed.

Q FACT: The first legal gay wedding ceremonies in the Netherlands took place on April 1, 2001. But how great a victory was it? Since 2001, the number of gay marriages in Holland has continued to fall (from 2,414 couples in 2001 to 1,210 in 2004) and only 6,000 of the Netherlands's 53,000 gay couples have gotten hitched. Lesbian couples represent half of these marriages, even though lesbians make up only 20 percent of the gay community.

But gay liberation has been a long, gradual process. Backtracking centuries, the city's history didn't really kick off until the 12th century, when farmers and fishermen tamed marshlands around the Amstel River (from which Amsterdam derives its name), introducing ditches and dykes of the wooden variety—butches would come later. While archaeological evidence suggests people strayed through the region in Roman times, no one actually stayed. Hardly surprising, considering the area's shifting lakes and swamps offered little to keep wandering tribes afloat.

Amsterdam's greatest expansion happened during the 17th century, a.k.a. its Golden Age, when the city dominated global sea trade. The first signs of

JACOB ISRAËL DE HAAN

DUTCH POET Jacob Israël de Haan (1881–
1924) earned disputable fame for *Pijpelijntjes*,
the first openly gay novel published in Dutch,
and later, as the object of political murder. Following the *Pijpelijntjes* scandal, de Haan married Dr. Johanna van Maarseveen, but the marriage ultimately failed and he left Amsterdam for
then-Palestine. There, the Jewish poet worked
as a correspondent for the leading Dutch newspaper *Algemeen Handelsblad,* but became increasingly critical of Zionism, and a potential
threat in what was already a political hotspot.
His controversial stance culminated in his murder by Zionist extremists in 1924. Today, a line
from one of de Haan's poems has been carved
onto Amsterdam's Homomonument. It reads:
"For Friendship such a Boundless Longing."

gay subculture began to emerge and an extensive
gay network evolved by 1730, when 289 sodomites
were arrested in neighboring Utrecht (thanks to a
male prostitute's confession). Morally shocked and
fearing divine retribution, Amsterdam's Calvinist
officials zealously executed sodomites, though straight
Amsterdammers weren't exactly outstanding examples
of decent behavior. Tagged "herring-picklers" and
"cheese-worms" by critics of the time, they were
renowned as drunkards, smokers, and (no surprise
when you combine vices) lewd. Amsterdam's first

WAR SUBVERSIVES

WE WERE Marked with a Big A and *After the War, You Have to Tell Everyone About the Dutch Gay Resistance Fighters*, are two films by Dr. Klaus Muller about gays in Nazi camps and the stories of gays/lesbians in the Dutch underground during WWII. For copies, contact the Washington State Holocaust Education Resource Center for more information (www. wsherc.org).

guidebook, published around this time, included the Red Light District—a bustling neighborhood of prostitutes and pornographers even then.

In fact, Amsterdammers were so vulgar, British and French monarchs used this very reason to declare war against their permissive neighbor as early as 1672. Neither succeeded until centuries later, when revolutionary France invaded Holland, capturing Amsterdam. The country was incorporated into the Napoleonic Empire in 1810 and Amsterdam fell under the jurisdiction of Napoleon's penal code, which had decriminalized homosexuality. For the next one hundred years—thanks to the French—homosexuality was considered fully legal.

In 1904, Holland's first gay novel appeared. Written by Jacob Israël de Haan, *Pijpelijntjes* was a thinly-veiled account of the author's promiscuous life and the book caused a huge scandal that cost de Haan his job as a primary school teacher. After the outrage erupted, gay and lesbian bar culture continued to develop slowly

ON DISPLAY

TAKING A step back in gay history, the Amsterdam Historical Museum has recreated the interior of the legendary 't Mandje, one of the city's first gay/lesbian watering holes run by the charismatic Bet van Beeren from 1927 to 1983 (the bar's actual exterior is preserved on Zeedijk Street). From a television behind the famed bar, Bet's surviving sister recounts stories of Bet's life, such as why there are so many clipped neckties dangling overhead.

in the city, but continued to be frequently and fiercely targeted by the police. In 1911, the Dutch Christian government passed article 248-bis, a decisive move increasing the gay age of consent to 21, effectively limiting Napoleon's code. Its passage, which was widely debated and never attained popular support, kick-started the burgeoning gay emancipation movement, which would continue far and beyond 1973, when the article was finally repealed.

During Nazi occupation, homosexuality was pushed underground and thousands of gays across Europe were deported to concentration camps.

After the war, a gay bar subculture openly emerged in Amsterdam, with lesbians, who were often former prostitutes, playing a key role—including legendary 't Mandje (The Little Basket) proprietor Bet van Beeren, a leather-clad, cigar-smoking dyke who heralded the lesbian movement long before Dykes on Bikes

CENTRE FOR CULTURE AND LEISURE

LAUNCHED IN 1946, the Centre for Culture and Leisure, or COC, headed the Dutch gay emancipation movement, culminating in its heyday during the sexual revolution. Originally established as a social club, which initiated Amsterdam's first gay and lesbian dance nights, the COC's real mission of promoting gay national interests soon became apparent. During the sixties, rising protest movements in almost every section of society spurred the COC into greater action. The organization worked toward broadening residence eligibility to gays, as well as effectively legalizing homosexuality in 1971. Today the COC is a volunteer-run organization with branches throughout the country. Its main concern now is gay integration, and the association provides information to schools, community centers, and the police, as well as actively responding to the media in order to fight discrimination.

In recent years, COC's Amsterdam branch has faced a turbulent period due to badly managed finances. To stay afloat, the organization canned regular dance nights—a huge blow to the gay community—and favored its administrative side (such as offering free legal advice). This has had a destructive domino effect. The COC used to run lesbian, Arabian, Gothic, and bear nights, but with no venue, many of these less-commercial events have folded altogether. What will happen with the COC remains to be seen, though one volunteer there commented, "Is the only way to find emancipation through discos? This is a serious question we're asking ourselves at the moment."

saw their first pair of training wheels. Bar culture developed slowly, however, due to constant, heavy police intervention and most queers met in tearooms, frequented by hustlers, instead.

In 1946, the COC (*Cultuur en Ontspannings-Centrum*) or Centre for Culture and Leisure, one of the world's oldest and largest gay rights organizations, was established. In its first years, the COC's cultural evenings were held under the supervision of the vice squad and many members joined secretly, using an alias to avoid recognition.

During the 1950s, a time of global prosperity and heightened consumerism, gay life openly blossomed in the city. The first gay hotels and many of the city's famous cafés and bars opened, including the De Odeon Kelder (DOK), the largest gay disco in the pre-Stonewall world. The COC also sponsored dance nights, highly popular with gay Amsterdammers up until 2005, when financial mismanagement put a sudden halt to parties. These dance nights created a radical change in the gay landscape and a monumental shift in gay and lesbian identity. No longer queers seeking sex with straights, gays could be openly homosexual and shed outdated butch/femme, effeminate/masculine roles. The DOK quickly became a meat-rack. In 1955, the city's oldest leather bar, the Argos, officially put its hide on the map and introduced the city's first darkroom. (A darkroom—literally a dark, poorly lit (if narrow) room made for anonymous sex—has since become a staple of the leather scene.)

During the sixties, Amsterdam's diverse gay bar culture became a major attraction and gay Europeans flocked to the city to openly enjoy pleasures denied to them at home. The sixties and seventies ushered in the sexual revolution and movements demanding widespread emancipation, from students and feminists to gays. The city's first gay sauna bolstered Amsterdam's reputation as a gay travel destination, openly gay bars with open windows proliferated throughout the city, and prominent gays and lesbians continued coming out of the closet.

As the gay subculture began to gain political foothold in the mid-seventies, a network of gay groups surfaced in trade unions, political parties, and universities. Radical faggots, or "potten" and "flickers," fought against heterosexual morality, opposing queer "normalization" by touting slogans like, "We want no place under the sun. We want a different beach." Lesbian activists played a particularly vital role in major protests, which flared over a citywide housing crisis, by squatting abandoned buildings and starting a number of women's cafés (see "Saarein II," Chapter 6), bookshops (see "Xantippe Unlimited," Chapter 4) and publishing houses, several of which survive today. The first gay parades were also held.

LESBIAN HERSTORY

SAY "DUTCH DYKE," and most people think of the little Dutch boy who stuck his chubby finger into one. But Amsterdam has a lively lesbian past. As early as 1632, 21-year-old Barbara van Brouwershaven was arrested for marrying her second wife Hilletje Jans, who inadvertently discovered her "husband" wasn't a man and called the authorities. In 1792, Bartha Schuurman was hung from the gallows for knifing her girlfriend's lover to death and many others were prosecuted for cross-dressing—to marry other women, find work as sailors, or pursue life outside their domestic sphere. If caught, they were sent to a "correction house" to do hard time with prostitutes, beggars, and thieves.

And, of course, there was the openly lesbian, gin-guzzling Bet van Beeren who opened the bar 't Mandje in 1927, in the disreputable Red Light District. One of the first biker dykes, van Beeren concealed weapons from the Nazis, sheltered Jews, and chased skirt until she died, when her body was laid out on the pool table of her bar. During the 1970s, radical lesbian groups organized Purple September to protest against male domination of the COC, and plastered slogans such as "Liever Lesbies" (we'd rather be lesbian) around town.

But despite a long-running presence in Amsterdam, lesbians have been marginalized compared to their gay brothers. Although *Saarein*, Amsterdam's first exclusively lesbian bar opened in 1978 *'t Mandje* served a mixed crowd), only a handful of lesbian-run venues currently exist. As is the case in other cities, Amsterdam's lesbian scene is somewhat hidden, often requiring the stealth of a private eye to track down women-only events, and today's generation seems rather complacent about its shagging rights. However, the annual Gay Pride celebration is a great equalizer, where lesbian participation remains strong year in, year out.

In 1982, a highly publicized queer bashing in neighboring Amsersfoort put gay protection high on the political agenda. When AIDS hit, the government readily cooperated with gay organizations, which immediately sent the alarm and became a crucial voice in raising awareness of the disease. The city insisted on comprehensive safer-sex education from grade school on up and rather than close sex venues down, the government decided to fund safe-sex parties and stock darkrooms and saunas with condoms. In 1987, the city unveiled the Homomonument, a sculptural tribute to acknowledge gays killed by the Nazis, but also including those persecuted throughout history. A first of its kind, the monument has attracted thousands of tourists over the years.

As the AIDS crisis calmed in the early nineties, the focus returned to sex, kinky parties, and outrageous gay nights at the RoXY and iT, both of which folded due to separate disasters in 1999, a year after same-sex partnerships became legally recognized. This was a turning point where sexual politics would become increasingly conservative.

In 2002, the assassination of openly gay politician Pim Fortuyn shocked the nation and rocked what had become a politically bland scene. Fortuyn, who was anti-immigration and labeled a far-right populist, had made his sexuality a positive issue, flaunting his taste for Maggie Thatcher's purses. Fortuyn's nationalist agenda to close Dutch borders angered many politicians and provoked the public, including the vegan animal rights activist who finally murdered him.

While Fortuyn's fears that Holland's permissive attitudes to drugs, sex, and homosexuality were being encroached upon by Muslim immigrants in the name of "religious freedom" caused widespread controversy (which continues today), they stimulated latent nationalism and ironically ushered in the conservative government that has since worked to curb what it sees as liberal laws. A case in point, Prime Minister Jan Peter Balkenende, when asked by an Indonesian student why the Netherlands allowed gay marriage, replied that he had voted against the legislation, offering no public support of his predecessors.

Today, gays have full equal status in the Netherlands. It's illegal to discriminate against job seekers on the basis of sexual orientation. The police advertise in the gay media for applicants, and the local police force even operates a network of gay police officers, the *Roze in het Blauw* (Pink in the Blue), to monitor gay-related crime. In 2001, the Netherlands made a

LOVE EXILES

"AMSTERDAM IS the capital of exile for gays and lesbians," says Martha McDevitt-Pugh, founder of Love Exiles, a foundation created in 2002 to support LGBT couples facing immigration issues in order to be together. McDevitt-Pugh, who started the organization while taking a self-expression course, also counts herself as a refugee. "I didn't have the choice to stay in my country on my own terms," says the California native, who remained in Holland to be with her Australian wife Lin. "And the more I got used to having all my rights, the less I wanted to go back to being a second-class citizen."

Holland is one of the few countries (there are 17 total) where same-sex partnerships are fully recognized. The Netherlands has taken the international lead on this issue, allowing gays and lesbians to sponsor their foreign partners as legal immigrants, and recognizes three forms of partnership: registered partnerships, those who cohabit, and marriage, which was legalized in 2001. "I like the Dutch smorgasbord approach to rights," says McDevitt-Pugh, "It's very individual—you can get married or not—although I personally think it's very daring to say you want to make something work for the rest of your life."

Thanks to McDevitt-Pugh, Love Exiles has played a role educating the public about issues same-sex binational couples and their families face. Of the future, says McDevitt-Pugh, "Love Exiles would like to globalize gay rights so other couples can have what we experience in the Netherlands. We'd like to see free movement for same-sex partners all over the world so we can feel free to be wherever we want to be." McDevitt-Pugh, for her part, is focusing her attention locally. Within the European Union, same-sex marriages are not recognized despite their Dutch legal status, meaning if a gay couple buys a home in France, neither partner can inherit it as a spouse. "I want to see the EU take this on," she says.

Comprehensive information can be found on its website (www.loveexiles.org) and local groups operate in Germany, Canada, England, and Australia.

landmark move becoming the first country to legalize same-sex marriage. Gays and lesbians can also adopt children, and several city council members are openly homosexual. However, in recent years, the evolving issue of homophobia within Holland's growing Muslim community has drawn many gay activists to the political right, which has used the dilemma to curb immigration, pitting minorities against each other.

Today gays in the Netherlands face an interesting time. They have fought—and won—full legal equality, but are now faced with the next step: promoting full social equality, something that cannot be easily legislated.

Kirsten Anderson, a Love Exile

MARRIED TO her Dutch partner since 2001, Kirsten Anderson, a California lawyer on the board of Love Exiles, felt she had no choice but to move to the Netherlands. "I had to come here or I wouldn't be with my partner; it's that simple," says Anderson, who (rather ironically) works with a San Francisco-based firm on U.S. immigration issues. "One thing most Americans don't understand is that immigration is a federal law. Even though Massachusetts recognizes same-sex civil unions, it doesn't give you the right to sponsor your partner. The Netherlands has been supporting same-sex immigration since the 1970s, so there really was no choice."

Anderson met her future wife at the NYC Gay Games in 1994, where they played badminton and Anderson lost. "She invited me to stay if I ever made it out to the Dutch Gay Games, which I did in '98. Then the relationship blossomed." After skyrocketing phone bills averaging $300/month, and several visits, Anderson decided to move. "I love

California, so it wasn't easy to change my life and give everything up—it had an enormous impact. Although it took some time to adjust to a new culture, I am happy to be with my wife, Jacqueline, in the Netherlands. There are far worse places to be a love exile than here and I am grateful that we can be together."

THE ADONIS CINEMA FLYING THE FLAG.

CHAPTER 2

The Basics

QUOTE

The Dutch live by the maxim "Live and let live."

SERIOUSLY THINKING about visiting Amsterdam? You're in good company. Once home to marshy grasslands, this cosmopolitan city is one of Europe's top ten tourist locales and home to multi-lingual, friendly Amsterdammers, who'll gladly show you the way—but only if you don't step into their bike path. The city is laid out in a series of concentric, U-shaped canals lined by snug streets with narrow, though impressive colonial houses. Amsterdam is very gay-friendly but the main neighborhoods parading the rainbow flag are the Reguliersdwarsstraat, home to splashy bars for the young-and-the-restless; the Amstel River, where locals croon to camp Dutch standards; and finally the Warmoesstraat, adjacent to the city's infamous Red Light District, where lusty leathermen like to linger.

Before arriving, or as last-minute reading aboard your flight, here are the basics.

When to Go

AS ANY Dutch weatherman will tell you, Amsterdam's climate is wet, windy, and variable. January and February are the coldest months with limited daylight (8 hours) and Dutch summers are mild—unless you consider the mid-60s humid as some locals do.

The Dutch have a saying: "God created the world, but the Dutch created Holland." About half the land in the Netherlands lies at or below sea level. Because there are few natural barriers, the maritime climate remains uniform throughout the country, so cloudy skies with rain are the norm. Just as New York City is a 24/7 metropolis constantly in motion, the skies over Holland are always shifting. What goes up—the massive evaporation from canals, rivers, arms of the sea, and extensive waterways—must inevitably come down.

A word to the wise: because it rains regularly year round, bad weather is impossible to avoid. So when is a good time to visit? Consider the sunnier summer months (May–August) when the rain is less likely to dampen your sightseeing efforts, not to mention your hair gel. Or, if you're set on camping out in a coffee shop, season is irrelevant—although there's definitely more seating in February.

What to Wear

IN HOLLAND, casualness is standard. The general Dutch aversion to showiness, based in Calvinist roots,

AVERAGE HIGH TEMPERATURES

JANUARY: 40°F	**JULY:** 72°F
FEBRUARY: 43°F	**AUGUST:** 72°F
MARCH: 49°F	**SEPTEMBER:** 67°F
APRIL: 56°F	**OCTOBER:** 58°F
MAY: 63°F	**NOVEMBER:** 49°F
JUNE: 68°F	**DECEMBER:** 43°F

means they feel safe playing dull and because most people still get from A to B via bike, stylish clothes are not a priority—but rain jackets are. Luckily, the gay community stands a slightly better chance when it comes to fashion. (Case in point, some Dutch Finance Ministry employees still wear white socks with dress shoes, a "style crime" that attracted lengthy discussion in 2004 after the BBC pressed for further investigation.) When it comes to what to wear, our best advice is this: As fresh airplane meat you're clearly going to stick out, so flaunt your homespun couture. Just remember to keep it rain-proof, so you'll stay warm and dry.

Q FACT: HOLLAND OR THE NETHERLANDS?

So, you've just arrived in Amsterdam but you're not really sure what country it's in—is it the Netherlands, Holland, or Dutch? While most outsiders call it Holland, the country is officially known as the Netherlands. Amsterdam itself lies in the province of North Holland, which is one of twelve provinces in the Netherlands. This is like saying London is in England, which is part of the United Kingdom. Dutch is the language, but the Dutch call it Nederlands, so if you're confused by now, you've got company.

When You Arrive

AMSTERDAM IS located nine miles by train from Schiphol Airport, the Netherland's main international airport and totally unpronounceable to outsiders (just think "ship hold" with a guttural *chhhhh* lodged in between). While taxis are available, they are also prohibitively expensive—Amsterdam rates rank amongst the highest in Europe at €1.50/half-mile regardless of time of day. Taking the train is a faster and cheaper alternative. All air passengers arrive in the Central hall, or Schiphol Plaza, where the train station also lies (just stroll beyond the first cafés facing the arrival hall and you'll see several ticket counters). The train tracks are situated directly below. For more information, check out the airport website: www.schiphol.nl or www.ns.nl (for the national train service).

For early morning or late-night arrivals, night trains travel once an hour to Amsterdam's Centraal Station and a one-way fare will put you out €3.60. Once at Centraal Station, several bus and tram lines are located directly in front. If taxis are your thing and you prefer door-to-door service directly from Schiphol, a trip to the city center runs €35.

CLUE

USING TRAINS

If you get on board without
buying a ticket, you could be
fined €35 plus the train fare for
the pleasure—even if you're a
confused, jetlagged tourist here
for the first time. Always buy
a ticket at the railway station
counter **before** entering the train.

Money

FORGET TRAVELERS' checks, cash, or personal
checks—all you really need here is a valid ATM card.
For plastic addicts, while major credit cards are widely
accepted, some hotels and shops impose a 5 percent
surcharge (or even more) to offset commissions, so
check before you charge. Charging or using your ATM
card always guarantees a good exchange rate, and ATM
(or *geldautomaat)* machines can be found throughout
the city, including the airport.

As a general rule cold hard cash is preferred, even for
large purchases, as the Dutch are prudent with money. A
sign from restaurant Hemelse Moeder bluntly sums up
the Dutch attitude to credit junkies and the cash poor:
"Use of credit cards is possible, but preferably not."

For those with foreign cash, the best place to

CALLING AMSTERDAM

exchange money and cash traveler's checks is the GWK (or *Grenswisselkantor*, open 24 hours a day in Centraal Station) or at any bank, but banks charge commission. Business hours differ from bank to bank. Most banks are open Tuesday to Friday from 9 am to 4 pm and on Mondays after 1 pm. They are closed on weekends.

Since January 1, 2002, the Euro (€) is the official currency of the Netherlands. It is divided in 100 cents. Coins come in 1, 2, 5, 10, 20, 50 cents; and 1 and 2 Euros (€). Notes come in 5, 10, 20, 50, 100, 200, and 500 Euros (€).

The current exchange rate is 1 USD = 0.788217 EUR or 1 EUR = 1.26869 USD. (For up-to-date currency rates, check out www.XE.com or www.x-rates.com.)

CLUE

XXX ACTION

Considering Amsterdam's freewheeling reputation, it seems appropriate the city's emblem has three Xs running through its center. Thought to be St. Andrew's crosses, they represent three moral virtues: compassion, resolution, and heroism (though a modern-day marketing campaign might pitch it differently).

Calculating

Don't be surprised if you catch locals still calculating things, especially expensive items, in *gulden* (or guilders, the retired, old-style currency). When the Euro was introduced in 2002, shopkeepers raised prices rather than make strict conversions, and your average *Nederlander*—who will have no problem going into a lengthy discussion about it—has been reluctant to embrace it.

Tipping

In Holland, don't feel obliged to leave a tip. A service charge is included in hotel, taxi, bar, café and restaurant bills, so what you see is what you pay. Most Amsterdammers, though, generally round up change to the nearest Euro.

Shop Hours

TO THE outsider, general business hours in the Dutch capital are a difficult, Byzantine system to understand. Most places are closed Sundays, and many don't reopen until late Monday afternoon although the rest of the week, business hours run roughly from 9 a.m. to 6:00 p.m. But…ask a shop employee something at 5:59 and you're likely to get a cold stare and a push toward the exit. Staying on a minute past clocking out time is complete anathema to the Dutch, who worship the separation between work and leisure. Thursdays, many stores stay open until 9 p.m., and *avondwinkels,* or night shops (which sell alcohol and food basics), stay open until midnight. In the tourist center near Leidseplein shops are usually open late night.

Bars open at various times throughout the afternoon and usually close at 1 a.m. during the week and 2 or 3 a.m. on the weekends. Clubs are often licensed until 5 a.m. and restaurants typically close around midnight.

Getting Around the City

AMSTERDAM IS a compact city and public transportation is easy to use. There's an extensive system of trams, buses, a modest subway and trains that operate until midnight, although several night buses run for 24-hour partygoers and insomniacs. Others get around by bike, taxi, or especially on foot. The city is ideal for walking.

But…before you step aboard, the city's public

CLUE

SAVING MONEY

Lunch and trains from the airport aside, Amsterdam can be an expensive city. Hotel rooms are not cheap (averaging between €100 and €125 a night) and taxis will eat your hard-earned money at a surprisingly accelerated rate. However, the city boasts flea markets such as the Albert Cuyp and Waterlooplein where you can find cheap (but fashionable) clothes, books, antiques, and souvenirs. Restaurants tend to be mid-range, though luxury options are available, but if you like to snack, Amsterdam is lined with kiosks and takeaway eateries where you'll find French fries, falafel, pizza slices, etc. The further away from the main tourist areas (the Red Light District, Dam Square, Rembrandtplein and Leidseplein) the cheaper it gets—whether it's hotels, pubs, restaurants, or the like.

transportation system uses the ubiquitous *strippenkaart*, or strip ticket, which must always be validated with a stamp. Tickets, cheaper when bought in advance, can be purchased at the GVB (that's the local transit authority or *Gemeentevervoerbedrijf*) kiosk across from Centraal Station. Post offices, supermarkets, and tobacconists also sell them or you can pay once you're aboard, but it's more expensive.

For more information, the GVB has an office across the tram tracks from Centraal Station (Tel. (+31) 0900 92 92, Stationsplein 10; 7 a.m.–9 p.m. Mon–Fri, 8 a.m.–9 p.m. Sat/Sun). Their website, www.gvb.nl, has extensive travel information in English.

Also, all transportation runs on a complicated zone system. Most tourists only travel within the Central zone, but rather than figure this out by yourself, ask for help. If you fail to stamp your *kaart* correctly, you could face a stiff fine—something prepared locals avoid.

Trains

Amsterdam's main train station is Centraal, which has regular, highly efficient connections throughout the country and to international destinations. Buy train tickets in advance at vending machines or at ticket offices at larger stations. Do *not* board without a ticket or you could face a hefty fine. Most tourists only use the train to travel to and from Schiphol Airport, and trains are an extremely popular form of transportation between cities.

Trams

Aside from bikes, trams are by far the most widely used form of transportation in Amsterdam. Quick, constant, dependable, clean, and frequent, there are seventeen tram lines running throughout the city, several of which terminate at Centraal Station. To use them, buy a punch card or *strippenkaart,* tell the driver where you're going and he or she will punch your card or tell you the fare.

Taxis

A good way to burn through your money, taxis are v-e-r-y expensive in Amsterdam. Unless you make a reservation or head toward a stand (*standplaats taxis*), flagging one down can be a Herculean challenge. To increase your chances, look for a lit taxi sign or dial the main number: (020) 677-77 77 while flailing at oncoming traffic.

Buses

While buses are mostly used in the outer suburbs or north of the city, there are roughly thirty lines that cover the same territory as trams. Board the bus at the front, show the driver your *strippenkaart* or buy one from him or her. Night buses run on nine different routes in the city, hourly during the week/half-hourly at the weekend, and are more expensive than day buses.

Subway

Mostly used by commuters, Amsterdam's subway system is small. There are only three lines, all terminating at Centraal Station, which run from 6 a.m. until midnight. For tickets use the strippenkart. In 2006, the city's municipal council courted vandals to wreck new subway trains to test whether they were "Amsterdam-idiot-proof." No word yet, but they're relatively safe. (For a map, click on www.amsterdam.info/transport/metro/.)

Bikes

Seven hundred and fifty thousand people live in Amsterdam with an estimated 600,000 bikes; it's clear what the city's most popular form of transportation is. But the extensive network of bike paths lining the roads isn't always as obvious—until you step into oncoming traffic. The Dutch ride aggressively, and will clang their bells impatiently as they try to evade motorcycles, delivery trucks, buses, trams, and, the most dangerous thing on the road, map-reading tourists. Bike capital of the world, Amsterdam should be viewed while sitting above whirring spokes. Cycling is the fastest way of getting around.

Want to go native and rent a bike? Rental companies require ID plus a cash or credit card deposit. Prices are for sturdy Dutch models with high handlebars, coaster foot breaks, thick tires, an even thicker lock and second lock for the rear wheel. Insurance is extra but you might need it if you fail to lock up properly. Approximately 80,000 bicycles are stolen in Amsterdam every year, so odds are not always in your favor. Before really hitting traffic, try practicing in Vondelpark, a gentler introduction to the streets.

BIKE CITY, Bloemgracht 68 – 70, Tel: +31 (0)20 626 37 21, www.bikecity.nl

DAMSTRAAT RENT-A-BIKE, Damstraat 20 – 22, Tel: +31 (0)20 625 50 29, www.bikes.nl

HOLLAND RENT-A-BIKE Damrak 247 (near Dam Square), Tel: +31 (0)20 622 32 07

MACBIKE, five separate locations, including Centraal Station and Leidseplein, Tel: +31 (0)20 620 09 85, www.macbike.nl

Q FACT: BIKER FRENZY For the Dutch, cycling is almost genetic. With 20,000 kilometers of designated bike paths, the Netherlands has made cycling a significant part of the national infrastructure and the country has one of the highest bike densities in the world. Its population of fifteen million owns 17 million bicycles and an estimated 3.4 million hop on for the daily commute. In Amsterdam, famous for its cycling hordes, 600,000 bicycles cruise the city. Each year, about 80,000 of them are stolen and 25,000 end up in the canals. This does little to deter the Dutch who see cycling as a solid form of sustainable transport.

Drug Policies

Think marijuana is legal in Holland? Actually, it's not. While Dutch drug policy makes a distinction between marijuana and hard drugs (e.g., heroin, cocaine), all drugs are considered illegal, though *using* drugs, paradoxically, is not. When it comes to dope, smoking within the confines of coffee shops, which are strictly regulated, is legal, but producing, possessing, or selling weed isn't—not that most tourists have the time or inclination. Marijuana's status is more "semi-legal" because the government, which actually quotes research conducted by America's Institute of Medicine, has found no evidence proving it's a "gateway" drug.

Confused? Does this still mean you can toke? Absolutely! The Dutch worldview is to leave tourists to their vices, but common etiquette is be discreet. If you smoke on the street, police will redirect you to the nearest coffee shop because—world-renowned reputation aside—most Dutch aren't big smokers. Ever heard of Heineken?

A lesser known cousin to coffee shops, smart drug shops offer a variety of "mind-enhancing" herbs. These include stimulants, sex enhancers, aphrodisiacs, energy drinks, post-indulgence recovery kits, and hallucinogens such as magic mushrooms. Some places even sell mushroom joints, and there is always a written explanation of what mind-altering effects to expect. When shopping, you'll find only fresh magic mushrooms available—dry ones are considered a psilocybin containing preparation (i.e., "processed") and therefore, illegal.

As a result of liberal drugs policy, the number of drug-related deaths in the Netherlands is the lowest in Europe, according to a study by the European Monitoring Centre for Drugs and Drug Addiction in Lisbon. As for weed, usage is also low, even lower than in United States (17% versus 34%). But marijuana policy could change. The Dutch government is being pressured by the EU to bring soft drugs policy in line with European legislation—effectively turning back the clock. New coffee shop permits are rarely given, so as coffee shops close, they are silently, but very systematically, dying.

Dutch Character

Just like Dutch houses with narrow façades hiding an expansive interior, the Dutch are modest and somewhat aloof. There's definitely more to them than first meets the eye, but you might have to knock several times before being let in. Intelligent, levelheaded, highly pragmatic and quick to speak their minds, they're an odd, paradoxical mix. Social liberals who are willing to experiment, but who ultimately shy away from confrontation, the Dutch are more conservative than they'd like to admit. But with a history built on consensus, it's not a total surprise. Without social agreement, Amsterdam would look more like Atlantis—you can't build an extensive network of dykes and canals on your own.

Still, born travelers focused on what lies beyond the horizon, the Dutch inherited open-mindedness from their seafaring forefathers who imported foreign ideas, products, and peoples creating a multicultural society (roughly 47 percent of the city's current residents come from immigrant families) that has drawn some of the world's most independent thinkers. Today, the Dutch are self-assured, worry little about what others think of them (because a Hollander is always right, comments simply bounce off), and generally live by the maxim "live and let live."

Gezellig

It might sound like a city, but *gezellig,* a word impossibly hard to translate, encompasses the very heart of Dutch culture. To the Dutch, *gezellig* is a priority as much as appearing on national TV is for Americans. So what does it mean? The guttural sounding adjective expresses warmth, coziness, good times, party spirit, and friendship and applies to people, places, and things. Some *gezellig* examples: a living room crammed with knick-knacks, laughing with friends over a bottle of good wine, a fluffy pink terrycloth robe, and Eurovision sing-a-longs at your favorite bar. The effectiveness of *gezellig* increases when cradling a cup of coffee and you'll never hear it mentioned with "upscale" in the same sentence.

Q FACT ON AMSTERDAM 1,498,205 inhabitants in Amsterdam and environs, 738,763 inhabitants in Amsterdam itself, 600,000 bicycles, 220,000 trees, 38,200 hotel beds, 6,800 16th–18th century houses and buildings, 2,500 houseboats, 1,281 bridges, 1,215 cafés and bars, 206 paintings by Van Gogh, 173 nationalities, 165 canals, 140 wax figures at Madame Tussaud's (including Robbie Williams!), 51 museums, 28 parks, 22 paintings by Rembrandt, 8 wooden drawbridges, 6 windmills, and 1 flower market.

A CUTE POOCH STANDS GUARD AT THE ENTRANCE TO THE
HOTEL NEW AMSTERDAM.

CHAPTER 3

Bedding Down

QUOTE

> Many hotels, like Dutch homes, are narrow buildings with steep stairs, which become even steeper after a few drinks.

IN AMSTERDAM, most gay hotels do not run in the five-star category. Their biggest selling point is location, location, location—as central to the nightlife as possible. Hotels like the Golden Bear, the city's first exclusively gay hotel, may only be one-star but their location is within prime spitting distance of gay nightlife. Amsterdam is compact, but staying outside the city center could force you to rely on Europe's most expensive taxis for late-night outings—and guaranteed, there are much better ways of spending your money.

Before deciding where to bed down, Amsterdam has four predominantly gay neighborhoods.

The popular *Amstel* district near *Rembrandtplein*, a terrace-lined square during the summertime, attracts middle-aged, local men who favor traditional sing-a-longs. There are many high-class hotels in the area or you can rent houseboats along the river.

The *Kerkstraat*, one of the city's oldest gay areas and also the most consistently crowded with tourists and straight locals (thanks to neighboring *Leidseplein*), is located near the museum quarter and just north of *Vondelpark* (http://hotels. gayamsterdam.com/gayhotels.php?area=kerk). There are many luxury hotels in the area, and most gay hotels are also close by.

The *Reguliersdwarsstraat*, Amsterdam's most trendy gay neighborhood especially for nightlife, is located near a handful of deluxe hotels, but most gay hotels are actually located farther afield (mainly, the other areas we've listed). This is never a quiet place as beautiful boys, businessmen, and local celebrities—who always love to be seen and heard—rub elbows (amongst other things) here.

Finally, the leather crowd gathers in the *Warmoestraat*, right in the middle of the bustling Red Light District, where hotels run from very basic to *ooh-la-la* deluxe. If you're looking for quiet here, forget getting any Zzzs—there's too much kink to keep you up and prowling.

Outside gay hotspots, Amsterdam's hotels are relaxed about same-sex couples and there's no need to be discreet requesting a queen-size bed. If you want to live it large, there are numerous boutique hotels such as the

THINGS TO KNOW BEFORE COMING

1. Amsterdam's status as a top tourist destination can sometimes turn finding a place to stay into a tough competition. While there are roughly 351 hotels in town, sometimes they all appear full, leaving the reservation-less grasping at their credit cards. Whenever you decide to go, book early.

2. Rooms can be small—surprising, considering the Dutch boast the tallest height average in the world, but this wasn't the case a century ago. Words like "broom closet" have been mentioned by unhappy guests so ask before arriving. Or don't be disappointed when—alas!—you hoped for something bigger.

3. Many hotels, like Dutch homes, are narrow buildings with steep stairs, which become even steeper after a few drinks. If you're an optimist, it just adds to the charm when you finally make it to the top.

4. The service industry in Holland, compared to the United States, can

be very second-rate. While the Dutch pride themselves on their directness/ lack of subtlety, when it comes to serving others, they're squeamish. Culturally, they've been brought up to expect they are equal in all situations, so asking a receptionist/bellhop/ waiter to actually serve you without making him feel bossed around is dancing an extremely fine line. Praise won't work—the Dutch are Calvinists—but critical comments, seen as a sign of intelligence, will. Be fussy. It will definitely get you further.

College or the Pulitzer, a *Conde Nast Traveler* favorite, where you can lay your shopping bags down for the night. Unfortunately, there are no lesbian hotels, but all gay hotels are lesbian-friendly.

The following list is roughly divided into neighborhoods, including some gay-friendly, not-to-be-missed accommodations.

Amstel Area

FLATMATES, Kruithuisstraat 18, Tel: +31 (0)20 620 15 45, www. Flatmates.nl. A 3-star option, Flatmates offers a variety of accommodation (apartments, studios, bed and breakfast) at different locations and rates. Choices range from a spacious two-bedroom apartment with roof terrace to a cozy, attractively furnished B&B with fresh cut flowers on arrival. More private than your average hotel, this is great value for the money. Rates vary but an average cost is €158 for a single, €178 for a double.

FRIENDSHIP B&B, Achtergracht 17 G, Tel: +31 (0)20 622 12 94, www.friendshipbnb.nl. Originally a barge for carrying cargo, this well-maintained houseboat sits on a quiet but central canal. If you're interested in living the life aquatic, there are two bedrooms, a large bathroom and fully equipped kitchen aboard, plus unlimited Internet access for cyberexplorations. The use of two bicycles is also included in the price. Rates are €110 per night for two people, but after three nights the price drops to €100. The longer the stay, the better the price, and it can get rather *gezellig,* or cozy, sitting on the water.

ITC HOTEL, Prinsengracht 1051, Tel: +31 (0)20 623 02 30, www.itc-hotel.com. While it's not clear what ITC stands for (perhaps Internet access). Tastefully facing a canal, the hotel is exclusively gay and lies on a quiet stretch in central Amsterdam. Rooms are clean and conservatively furnished, with 24-hour gay TV access and if that works your appetite up, there's a generous breakfast buffet below. Singles run €55 and doubles €75. A 5 percent city tax also applies.

Kerkstraat

AERO, Kerkstraat 49, Tel: +31 (0)20 622 77 28, www. aerohotel.nl. A popular, small hotel off the bustling

TITLE

tourist strip, the Aero's situated in the Art Deco Liberty Building, considered a local monument. Currently under renovation, it offers clean and simple rooms, not all with private facilities. On one side of the hotel you'll find the porn video rental shop Bronx, on the other, Camp Café, where the hotel serves breakfast—making this one of the most convenient places in the known universe. Singles run €45, doubles €100.

AMISTAD, Kerkstraat 42, Tel: +31 (0)20 624 80 74, www. amistad.nl. Renovated, with a Gay Internet Lounge to boot, this is one of Amsterdam's oldest gay hotels. Rooms are stylish and smart and the hotel's motto "Sleep with us!" is no understatement—breakfast is sleepily served until 1 pm, so you can catch your beauty sleep. Customers are encouraged to relax, take their pants off, and enjoy staring at the art—or preferably, the ceiling. Rooms also contain phone,

TV, Internet access, coffee machine, etc. Basic singles are €65, deluxe singles €99. Standard doubles are €80, deluxe €130.

GOLDEN BEAR, Kerkstraat 37, Tel: + 31 (0)20 624 47 85, www.goldenbear.nl. This is Amsterdam's oldest gay hotel. Close enough to the Warmoesstraat to stagger back after a night spent on all fours, the hotel has colorful, attractive rooms with WiFi, phones, etc., and a daunting staircase leading to Room 25. Leather and, of course, bear-friendly, the hotel also arranges canal boat excursions and city tours led by local journalist Hans Tulleners, who knows a good almshouse when he sees one. Rooms run from €69 for a standard single to €99 for a double. Breakfast included in room rates.

Not exactly Amstel, but close by

CAKE UNDER MY PILLOW, Ferdinand Bolstraat 10, Tel: +31 (0)20 751 09 36, www.cakeundermypillow.com. Tourists—let them eat cake! Set in a fully-renovated 19th-century merchants building, this adorable B&B boasts large, sunny windows, charming rooms, and complimentary breakfast from the duo who also own Taart van m'n Tante, Amsterdam's premiere patisserie, which is located directly below. Forget watching your waistline, in addition to the café's mouth-watering cakes, the B&B is also close to a variety of excellent eating joints in de Pijp neighborhood. You might be able to work the calories off on your king-sized bed, though… Rooms from €80 to €150 (+5% tourist tax).

ORFEO, Leidsekruisstraat 14, Tel: +31 (0)20 623 13 47, www.hotelorfeo.com. A favorite with leather boys and centrally located between Kerkstraat and Reguliersdwarsstraat, Orfeo is Amsterdam's largest exclusively gay male hotel. Paradoxically, rooms are basic and small—think college dorm—but all come with TV, phone, and minibar. Complimentary (prepare yourself) Dutch breakfast is served in the hotel's new restaurant, Popa Pasta, which is actually Italian. Go figure. Single rooms cost €50 during high season, doubles cost €75. Threesomes—oops, that's triples—are also available.

QUENTIN, Leidsekade 89, Tel: +31 (0)20 626 21 87, www. quentinhotels.com. What other hotel would display a giant Keith Richards painting to welcome guests? Small and friendly, the Quentin caters mainly to gays and lesbians, and rumor has it, the Paradiso nightclub—a converted church, considered Amsterdam's temple of modern music—lodges visiting bands here, lending it a certain "might-spot-a-rockstar" appeal. An art deco reception and 50 well-kept rooms also keep clients coming. The hotel is also popular with lesbians. Rates: single €35–€80; double €55–€150, depending on season.

Warmoesstraat Area

ANCO HOTEL, Oudezijdsvoorburgwal 55, Tel: +31 (0)20 624 11 26, www.ancohotel.nl. A low-key hotel for leather right in the center, the Anco lies just a few blocks from the Warmoestraat. Men-only, in a renovated building dating back to 1640, it offers spotless singles, doubles, three–four bed dorms with shared amenities, and a studio with a small kitchen for those requiring more leg space. Singles cost €65 and doubles run €90. TV, continental breakfast inclusive in price, major credit cards accepted.

BLACK TULIP, Geldersekade 16, Tel: +31 (0)20 427 09 33, www.blacktulip.nl. A well-established, upmarket hotel with beautiful canal views, it's hard to say why leathermen flock here. Is it the chic, well-equipped (TV/CD/DVD, WiFi, minibar/fridge, etc.) rooms or the hotel's collection of slings, hoists, bondage chairs, hooks, and leather bedcovers that customers can reserve to fetter their fetters unfettered? Singles run €115, doubles €125; multiple function bondage-equipped stays cost more—but you're worth it. Rates inclusive of local tax and breakfast buffet.

CENTRE APARTMENTS, Heintje Hoeksteeg 27, Tel: +31 (0)20 627 25 03, www.gay-apartments-amsterdam.nl. For those wanting the personal touch, CA offers studios and apartments, both fully self-catering (i.e., own kitchen/microwave, though no phones) and all stylistically different, a short stroll away from Dam Square and the cruising stretch. Founders Gerard and Cris meet and greet at the front door (just choose a language—they speak six). Studios cost €125/person, an apartment for two runs €140, with an extra charge for laundry service. Minimum three-night stay.

STABLEMASTER, Warmoesstraat 23, Tel: +31 (0)20 625 01 48, www.stablemaster.nl. This small, no-frills hotel offers clean accommodation and sits directly above Stablemaster leather bar, home to the popular (almost nightly) Jack Off Party. The hotel, in the middle of the Red Light District, caters to the bar's clientele, making it exclusively male. Singles cost €65;

doubles €95; and apartments, with TV, refrigerator, and coffee maker, run €150.

THE WINSTON, Warmoesstraat 123, Tel: +31 (0)20 623 13 80, www.winston.nl. Super edgy, cheap, and artistic, the Winston's not gay, but it's on the main leather stretch and just as streetwise as its neighbors. Each hotel room has been designed differently from artists around the globe—everything from Polaroid wallpaper to Gothic-inspired chambers—which makes for a unique budget experience. A word of warning: the Winston tends to be loud. There's a bar downstairs and next door is Club Winston Kingdom, which hosts DJs every night, so better to roll in after last call than expect a deep beauty sleep. The hotel offers singles, doubles, triples, quads, and dorm rooms. Singles cost €55, doubles €70.

Close by, but not exactly in Warmoestraat

BARANGAY, Droogbak 15a, Tel: + 31 (0)62 504 54 32, www.barangay.nl. With a gay-sounding name (it actually means "small village" in Filipino) and owners who definitely are, the hotel boasts Amsterdam's only true tropical hideaway. The decor—tribal masks, wicker walls, orchids, palms, and more wicker furniture—smacks of former colonial days, where you're served breakfast in bed. Owners Wimmo and Godwin, or God, as he is called by friends, have run Barangay since 1999, and maintain clean, non-smoking rooms. Smoking is permitted on the patio. During peak season, rooms run from €99 to €129 per night.

THE EEL HOUSE, Tweede Lindendwarsstraat 21, Tel: +31 (0)20 330 05 44, www.eelhouse.nl. Named after the Amsterdam pastime of eel-baiting (stringing a greased, live eel on a rope that boat-goers would then try to grab) but f-a-r from slimy, this small, two-roomed guesthouse is owned by a Dutch-American gay couple. Both rooms include a queen-sized bed, built-in wardrobe, dishes, lazy chair, and minibar (also WiFi, TV/radio/CD, fridge—get the picture? Totally plush!) and run €90–€120 per night double occupancy. This is the perfect place for baiting your own catch, greasing him, and taking a tour of the ceiling.

MAES B&B, Herenstraat 26, Tel: +31 (0)20 427 51 65, www.bedandbreakfastamsterdam.com. Maes is one of the city's first B&Bs, well-known for its pleasant, feels-like-your-mother's-house ambience. Named after famous Dutch painter Nicolaas Maes, the hotel itself is exceedingly comfortable, with large bathrooms, a maze of staircases leading into attractive rooms, and sits on a quiet, well-located street. If the smell of fresh croissants in the morning is the only thing to get you moving before happy hour, you're in luck. Owners Ken Harrison and partner Vladmir Melnikov also run **Herenstraat** ("Gentleman's Street") **B&B** two doors down. Like Maes, they offer both rooms and apartments, tastefully decorated and slightly more masculine in flavor. All rooms are nonsmoking. Prices run from roughly €90 single to €130 for double at both B&Bs.

HOTEL NEW AMSTERDAM, Herengracht 13-19, Tel: +31 (0)20 522 23 45, www.hotelnewamsterdam.nl. On edge of the Jordaan neighborhood, the formerly-named New York hotel is chic. Rooms are spacious, clean, stylish, and offer the kind of minimalist aesthetic (simplicity leading to richness) that Japanese designers would go ga-ga for. Gay owned and straight friendly, with fabulous views of the Herengracht, this is a thinking-man's love lair. From €85 to €120 per night.

SUNHEAD OF 1617, Herengracht 152, Tel: +31 (0)20 626 18 09, www.sunhead.com. Built in—guess—1617, this B&B sits on the Herengracht or Gentleman's Canal, the most prominent of Amsterdam's 17th century canals. The building, considered a national monument, has two spacious rooms with exposed wooden beams, complete bathrooms, fridge, microwave, and TV. WiFi is also available but it's so quiet and cozy here, you're more likely to catnap than cavort through gay websites. Rates from €99 to €129 (including breakfast and taxes).

4 and 5 Star Hotels

THE COLLEGE HOTEL, Roelof Hartstraat 1, Tel: +31 (0)20 571 15 11, www.thecollegehotel.com (located near Museumplein in the Amstel neighborhood.) A trainee hotel for hotel, bakery, and tourism students, the College is run by late teens who would much rather be outside smoking a cigarette and text-messaging their mates than doing anything remotely resembling work. Having said that, the hotel, which was actually built as a school back in 1895, has been so beautifully renovated that—indolent mall youth aside—most people come back for more. What's on offer? Spacious suites; oversized beds; tall, elegant ceilings; and a lobby that is simply gorgeous. If you can ignore typical Dutch service, it's worth every well-earned Euro. Rates €205 for a superior single, €235 for a superior double.

THE DYLAN HOTEL, Keizersgracht 384, Tel: +31 (0)20 530 20 10, www.dylanamsterdam.com (located between Kerkstraat and Reguliersdwarsstraat). Sitting on Keizersgracht, one of the city's most famous canals, this 17th-century former theater has 41 stylish rooms in six different motifs, ranging from elegant to exotic. Most include a mix of oversize four-poster beds, sumptuous window treatments and limestone bathtubs. In so many words, its rich, superstar extravagance would make Barbra Streisand (remember *Architectural Digest*, May 1978, Vol. 35, no. 4) eat her heart out. A standard single is €260, a double €420, and a suite runs €1,490/night.

LLOYD HOTEL & CULTURAL EMBASSY, Oostelijke Handelskade 34, Tel: +31 (0)20 561 36 36, www. lloydhotel.com (located east of Centraal Station). Located in the fashionable Eastern Docklands, Lloyd's 4 and 5 star suites, designed by renowned Rotterdam architecture firm MVRDV (but don't try to pronounce it), emphasize tall, open spaces. Harbor views mingle with unconventional décor, and special features can include a polystyrene bathroom, 13-foot beds, grand pianos, or soundproofing for the über-sensitive. Kitchen access also allows visitors to cook if they wish. Prices vary from €95 to €295.

HOTEL PULITZER, Prinsengracht 315-331, Tel: + 31 (0)20 523 52 35, www.pulitzer.nl. This historical hotel near Dam Square is really 25 restored canal houses seamlessly integrated. With 230 rooms, meeting rooms ,and even an art gallery, it boasts a formal, Old World ambience. Rooms are decorated with heavy wood furniture and thick curtains—either elegant or stuffy, depending on your taste—and each is unique in design. Rooms run from €230 to € 335 for an executive room.

For Lesbians

AMSTERDAM HAS two women-only B&Bs, though they are not exclusively lesbian.

JOHANNA'S BED AND BREAKFAST, Hogendorpplein 62, Tel: +31 (0)20 684 85 96, home.planet.nl/ ~johannas/index.htm. Johanna's clean, reasonably priced rooms are somewhat plain and homely, but the neighborhood is excellent to wander through. Located in the west of Amsterdam near the Westergasfabriek, a "culture park" full of creative businesses, bars, and cafés, the B&B doesn't permit smoking or alcohol—you'll have to carry it back in your stomach. Room rates are €45–€65.

LILIANE'S HOME, Sarphatistraat 119, Tel: +31 (0)20 627 40 06. Situated in a gay-friendly neighborhood, this private home offers accommodation exclusively to women. Rooms include TV, fridge, books to read, and for breakfast, a basket of goodies delivered to your door. Gay boys are only allowed in two days a year—on Queen's Day and New Year's, when the number of female clients dip. Rates are €85 (single), €110 (double), €120 (double with private bathroom, balcony, and kitchen).

ROB LEATHER ON WARMOESTRAAT. DON'T MIND THE BARS, BOYS, COME ON IN.

CHAPTER 4

Shopping and More

> You walk through Amsterdam and see thousands of them, erect, darkish purple, with a triple-X shaft: *Amsterdammertjes*.

IN AMSTERDAM, whatever your fetish, guaranteed there's a shop selling it somewhere. That's because the Dutch are natural-born mercantilists with a ready eye for the next niche—and unapologetic gay shoppers with a penchant for plastic (credit or debit cards, not necessarily PVC), naturally fit the bill.

Amsterdam is a shopper's paradise. The Dutch made an empire stuffing their coffers with global goods, trading with all corners of the world, and the city today offers everything from upscale, highly specialized designer boutiques to bustling, year-round flea markets filled with merchandise a la Salvation Armani. Throw in antiques, postmillennial couture, Bakelite pudding molds, and size 46 pumps and you'll have hit but the tip of the proverbial consumerist iceberg.

When it comes to gay-specific shops, they're scattered across town, with some displaying a rainbow flag, others not. Outside the Warmoestraat in the Red Light District, the largest concentration of specialty and fashion shops (though not necessarily gay) are in the Negen Straatjes, or "nine little streets," a two-minute walk from Dam Square. There's also shopping at the Waterlooplein flea market and Albert Cuyp, the city's largest, busiest daily market that has been running for one hundred years.

Whatever you're looking for, you're sure to find it in Amsterdam.

Fetish Fashion

ABSOLUTE DANNY, Oudezijds Achterburgwal 78, Tel: +31 (0)20 421 09 15, www.absolutedanny.com. Across from Casa Rosso, known for its live sex shows, this fetish shop caters to men and women, though its latex, rubber, and lycra stock focus primarily on female customers (unless you're a submissive guy recently ordered into frilly briefs). Run by Danny Linden, who designs some of the gear herself, the shop is respected by professional Dominas and has a very straight-up, no-nonsense attitude when it comes to serving pervy needs. Danny organizes kinky parties in cooperation with Wasteland (one of Europe's largest kinky events) for those unself-respecting slaves who want to perform a public boot licking. She also runs a designer hotel for S&M. Just ask—no, *demand!*—information at the front desk.

BIG SHOE, Leliegracht 12, Tel: +31 (0)20 622 66 45, www.bigshoe.nl. Started by Marjan Kouw, whose feet hit size 46 (size 11.5 men's in the States) by her 12th birthday (due to Amazonian lineage or eating hearty Dutch *stampot*, we'll never know), Big Shoe takes itself literally—by selling big shoes. A paradise for those seeking gigantic girlie pumps, long boots, sandals, oversized ballet shoes, or various foot coverings resembling small hover craft, the store is definitely worth taking a look for size queens who really need it queen-sized.

BLACK BODY, Lijnbaansgracht 292, Tel: +31 (0)20 626 25 53, www.blackbody.nl. A well-known leather and rubber shop that boasts over 500 different styles of clothing, Black Body offers everything from socks, body bags, and britches to complete, made-to-order suits. They also offer toys, gizmos, poppers, and other goodies meant to fuel your fetish fantasies—including Primepork DVDs and zippers guaranteed to withstand thousands of prying fingers.

CONDOMERIE, Warmoesstraat 141, Tel: +31 (0)20 627 41 74, www.condomerie.com. So many condoms, so little time… Perfectly positioned on the edge of the Red Light District, the Condomerie makes good on its name with its stock of flavored, ribbed, and colored prophylactics for busy boys out shopping. Since its opening in 1987, the shop has pushed a safe-sex message alongside hundreds of products—such as United Colors of Benetton for boudoir fashionistas, Durex's "Chocolate" for late-night snackers, "Goliath" for those of colossal stature, and Madonna, for material girls who certainly aren't virgins. The shop provides information on everything from condom history (those former lambs' bladder models), to a measuring system—because size matters when you're looking for something snug.

FEMALE AND PARTNERS, Spuistraat 100, Tel: +31 (0)20 420 11 19, www.femaleandpartners.nl. Women know what women want, according to the shop's owners Ellen and Esther, and in Amsterdam, women want erotic designer lingerie, leather and rubber fetish gear, Pocket Rockets, Double Studs, and other items whose names confuse until you find the "On" switch. A well-maintained, friendly shop that's bright and far from seedy, it's located right next door to a smart shop—so if the basket of 50 percent off PVC thongs isn't aphrodisiac enough, you can hop next door to the smart shop for a herbal 69 fix.

MANTALK, Reguliersdwarsstraat 39, Tel: +31 (0)20 627 25 25. A spotless, bright shop carrying swimwear and a wide array of colorful undergear, Mantalk is the prefect place to find something you'd later love to take off. It's so hygienic and light inside, the store has all the ambience of a dentist's office, but it's all done to highlight the merchandise, which is more contemporary and clean than what you'll find in de Stringslip down the street.

DE MASK, Zeedijk 64, Tel: +31 (0)20 620 56 03, www.demask.com. If tottering from the heady heights of latex heels is your favorite way of delivering degradation, this is the shop for you. From PVC leotards and rubber panties to leather, buckled corsets, and suspension body bags, De Mask is serious about toilet training—or whatever it is you want your rubber boy to do. With a dressed-to-impress, informative staff and reasonable prices, this low-key, stylish shop has a great deal to offer—the only deprivation you'll experience here is leaving without buying so much as a collar. Shops also open in New York City, Dortmund, and Munich.

MR. B, Warmoestraat 89, Tel: +31 (0)20 422 00 03, www.misterb.nl. Tucked between leather bars, Mr. B's is big on its Bs: bondage, belts, boots, and butt plugs (the booty, or bounty, comes later—once you've trapped it). From its provocative window display to a selection of highly polished steel anal bolts and juggernaut butt plugs (which could easily sidetrack flights heading towards Schiphol), the shop draws in gay men, clients sporting enough tattoos to challenge the best inner-city mural, and curious tourists alike. Well-stocked with paddles, truncheons, harnesses, leather pants, and erotic toys, Mr. B does serious business while remaining friendly and inviting. The staff here is approachable and will not flinch when newcomers ask, "Er, what's this for exactly?"

DE NIEUWE KLEREN VAN DE KEIZER, Runstraat 29, Tel: +31 (0)20 422 68 95, www.denieuweklerenvandekeizer.nl. Also known as DNKVDK or, in English, the Emperor's New Clothes, this shop specializes in a wide array of club wear, street wear, and sportswear, including T-shirts from Men by Men, Priape, and Aerosol, and Mundo Unico underwear if you're looking for something from the waist down. Clothing is displayed by color, making it easy to find what you want and a 50 percent-off rack features prominently near the entrance. Unlike the scoundrels in Hans Christian Andersen's story, the staff here gives an honest opinion—they're Dutch after all. The threads are costly, but you can put the dentist off another month, *toch?*

ROB, Warmoestraat 32 and Weteringschans 253, Tel: +31 (0)20 428 30 00. www.rob.nl. Amsterdam's oldest leather emporium, Rob offers leather, latex, and perverse accessories on three fully-stocked floors and has expanded its reign of terror to branches in Berlin, London, Manchester, Paris, and Zurich. With a smaller accessories store in the Red Light District, Rob gives *Amsterdammertjes* (the city's phallic, steel sidewalk posts) a real run for the money. Lubes, harnesses, poppers, videos, and such paraphernalia also available but don't stare fixatedly at toys or pick them all up—or you'll cause a real sneer from the sales clerk.

ROBIN AND RIK, Runstraat 30, Tel: +31 (0)20 627 89 24. Custom fit leather feels so goooooood! A small shop that makes leather clothing, Robin and Rik is a boutique shop that has been making local leather boys happy for ages.

THE SHIRT SHOP, Reguliersdwarsstraat 64, Tel: +31 (0)20 423 20 88. For boys in need of T-shirts 7 days a week (or tourists avoiding laundry), the shop sells tight-fitting tees and shirts to help beauties flaunt their gym-given stuff. With two floors of crammed, colorful racks, only the very strong or those who left their American Express at home can resist leaving empty-handed.

STRAVERS, Overtoom 139, Tel: +31 (0)20 616 99 73. For those who need boots made for walking, rather than an exercise in Chinese foot binding, Stravers stocks ladies sizes up to 47 and men's up to 53 (USA size 13.5 and 19, respectively). Although the merchandise is plain and rather pricey, the store offers a practical solution for oversized boys.

DE STRINGSLIP, Reguliersdwarsstraat 59, Tel: +31 (0)20 625 64 44, www.stringslip.com. Just behind the Flower Market but offering merchandise for a whole different set of bulbs, the shop carries a variety of men's lingerie, and stocks products running from A to Z: from designer label thongs and briefs to poppers, leather S&M accessories (most of which appear in the window), and party tickets. A relaxed, everything kind of shop open everyday of the week, this gay 7–11 could turn even bigger profits if it got a liquor license—but for now, you'll have to order your beer across the street.

STOUT, Berenstraat 9, Tel: +31 (0)20 620 16 76, www. stoutinternational.com. Naughty lingerie for girls who like spending their Mama's money, Stout also has an unabashed collection of erotic jewelry, sensual oils, crystal dildos, and all the makings for a Beverly Hills 90210 grrls sleepover party. Stout means naughty in Dutch and incorporates the English sense of being robust—witness the dildos—and the store's merchandise reflects this sentiment in an ever-so-feminine way. For fashion that's sexy, stylish, and oh sooooo expensive, it's worth exploring if only to ditch that old flannel nightgown.

VAN RAVENSTEIN, Keizersgracht 359, Tel; +31 (0)20 639 00 67. In a city full of designers, Van Ravenstein's boutique offers cutting-edge fashion at its best.

The shop carries ready-to-wear from Holland's celebrated fashion duo Viktor & Rolf, seasonal lines from top Belgian designers such as Dries van Noten. But it's really V&R's fashion, frequently inspired by Dutch farmers and heralded as both idiosyncratic and smartly pragmatic (in other words: Dutch), that's worth the visit.

XARINA, Singel 416, Tel: +31 (0)20 624 63 83, www. xarina.nl. A store for high-class fetishists, dominant goddesses looking to outfit their subs and libertines ready to kick out some cash, Xarina carries colorful latex corsets, mini-dresses, gowns, and exclusive, tailor-made designs. For those who want to play risqué while looking like something the Emperor dragged in, this is the place to shop.

Books

THE AMERICAN BOOK CENTER (ABC), Spui 12, Tel: +31 (0)20 625 55 37, www.abc.nl. Europe's biggest English-language bookseller, ABC is a typical American enterprise. Founded in 1972 by two expats vending erotic magazines (who says smut doesn't sell) the store grew into a Dutch Amazon for English speakers. Packed on three floors with travel guides, U.S. periodicals, and an extensive gay and lesbian section housed in the basement, ABC also hosts seminars and workshops. For gay porn, ABC is limited, but as a general resource for information on Amsterdam, it really can't be beaten.

INTERMALE, Spuistraat 251, Tel: +31 (0) 20 625 00 09, www.intermale.nl. Amsterdam's largest bookstore

AMSTERDAMMERTJES

YOU WALK through Amsterdam and see thousands of them, erect, darkish purple, with a triple-X shaft: *Amsterdammertjes*. These steel sidewalk posts are meant to protect pedestrians from moving traffic but pose a greater threat to male anatomy thanks to their scrotum-tackling height (well, unless you're a tall Dutch man). Considered synonymous with the city, Amsterdammertjes were first introduced in 1972 but caused a greater effect on postcards than anything remotely connected to traffic. While the city toys with the idea of removing them from time to time, there seems to be greater inclination to mount them (witness the postcards) or ignore them all together (witness the damaged ones cars have backed into).

devoted entirely to gay male literature (not a euphemism for visual whacking-off material, which it also carries), Intermale has a large selection of books in English, Dutch, German, and French, ranging from the latest bestsellers to '60s retro porn where guys really let their hair—and there's a lot of it—down. Odd books, such as "A Natural Lizard Activity" about teenaged Kim and his dope-smoking Mom, might catch your attention, or rarer items displayed in the shop's antiquarian case. Either way, the selection here gives a refreshing spin on the term "well-stocked."

BUTT MAGAZINE

JOURNALISTS GERT JONKERS and Jop van Bennekom—both uncut, blond Dutch boys—founded *Butt* magazine (which is carried at Vrolijk) in 2001. Highly successful, the quarterly magazine by and for gay men has attempted to keep gay sex exciting and real. "We wanted to put the sex back in homosexuality," says Jonkers, who has avoided splaying models and actors across *Butt*'s pages, preferring to focus instead on real men and their real-life sex stories. But, he warns, the magazine's not wank material. "If you want to get off, you should go to a gay peep show because *Butt* is something to take home and digest."

The magazine offers engaging interviews with the likes of Christopher Ciccione, Paul Rutherford, and Casey Spooner, as well as covering the goings-on of porn stars, filmmakers, and even an auto-fellatio superstar. "Because Jop and I are journalists, we're intrigued by reality, not fiction," says Jonkers. "We'd talk to friends who'd had great sex, or hear a story about how some bartender was a great painter but there was no platform to express this before. So we created *Butt* and discovered like-minded gays," he says, adding, "and that's the greatest surprise—there are lots of guys out there interested in what we have to say."

VROLIJK, Paleisstraat 135, Tel: +31 (0)20 623 51 42, www.vrolijk.nu. Said to be Holland's largest gay and lesbian bookstore, Vrolijk has a huge selection of erotica, self-help books, literature, travel guides, magazines, and then some packed into two crowded floors. One side of the store is devoted to boys, the other to girls (a gesture just short of painting the walls pink and blue) and there's an extensive DVD collection housed on the second floor—also split into girls (erotica) and boys (forget-the-storyline porn). Feel free to venture to the other side of the shop though.

VROUWENINDRUK, Westermarkt 5, Tel: +31 (0)20 624 50 03, www.xs4all.nl/~vind. For those in love with books and the feel, smell, and sight of yellowing, dog-eared pages, this bookshop is Nirvana. Directly across from the Homomonument, Vrouwenindruk offers a large section of contemporary and rare English, French, Dutch, and German titles, not to mention an extensive lesbian and feminist collection. Books by and about women spanning history, travel, and fiction, ranging from recent to secondhand alike are mixed thoroughly together on crammed bookshelves, while others sit in cardboard boxes and bulging shopping bags. Coming here could be an all-day shopping expedition for dedicated bookworms.

XANTIPPE UNLIMITED, Prinsengracht 290, Tel: +31 (0)20 623 58 54, www.xantipe.nl. A lesbian feminist bookstore that had a makeover and decided to become more general, Xantippe stocks books ranging from art, travel, literature, and cookery to books for children. There's a wide selection of international women's magazines, a comprehensive women's studies section, and classical lesbian literature is stocked in the very back—making it seem as if the store is closeting itself. Still, there's a great selection in this very attractive store.

Gifts

BUTLER'S, Runstraat 22, Tel: +31 (0)20 676 47 60. For those who really like to splurge, Butler's, which carries exclusive home products, is the place for mission accomplished. The snug, sweet-smelling store stocks bedding, pillows, dishes, bathrobes, candles, and other home accessories by Missoni, Culti, Boudoir, Gunther Lambert, and Vivis, and acts as a luxury magnet for gay passerbys who suffer from weakening shopping resolve. "Hmm, coffee, tea, or *me*?"

DOM, Spuistraat 281, Tel: +31 (0)20 428 55 44, www. dom-ck.com. Dom is the perfect place to find stuff you never thought you needed—from kitsch, dildo-shaped soap, and pistol-shaped hairdryers to gaudy chandelier ornaments. Sporting an Asia-meets-Eurotrash sensibility when it comes to design, the shop is brimming with tasteful and reasonably priced home décor ideas. While the trendy young staff flits about hurriedly, constantly stocking and reorganizing shelves, there's little hurry to actually serve waiting customers—making customers who do want to buy something feel like they've just crashed a house party and demanded beer.

GIRLS LIKE US

ONE OF the freshest additions to Amsterdam's lesbian scene, *Girls Like Us* (GLU) magazine was created by Jessica Gysel and Kathrin Hero to showcase contemporary lesbians. "I hope to change people's perceptions of lesbians, move away from the butch/femme stereotypes and show a more intelligent, creative, and humorous side of our identity," says Gysel, who also runs a marketing innovation agency.

GLU covers topics running the gamut from girls who become boys, skaters, and dyke music icons, to documented material from Amsterdam's own gay and lesbian archive. But unlike traditional text-heavy lesbian magazines of yore, GLU is glossy, with full-color photo spreads. Says Gysel, who's not interested in labeling her magazine, "We're trying to break down clichés because most people, including lesbians, tend to put themselves in a box. GLU is meant to be subversive, but we do it in a playful, sincere way."

FROZEN FOUNTAIN, Prinsengracht 629, Tel: +31 (0)20 622 93 75, www.frozenfountain.nl. A sprawling, trend-setting shop/gallery/interior design emporium that sells contemporary Dutch furniture and home accessories, FF is as much a furniture store as a revolving testament to emerging local design. Run by Dick Dankers and Cok de Rooy (snicker, snicker) this is a first-stop shop for modern furniture from the likes of Driade, Depadova, and Moroso. The store features hip, colorful, and—predictably—expensive items ranging from lampshades to sofas, and draws a constant stream of customers who stroll slowly through the store, silently calculating. FF regularly organizes expos that focus on rising Dutch stars, whose work is ingenious, quirky, and yet down-to-earth—in other words, terribly Dutch.

GALLERY FAUBOURG, Overtoom 426, Tel: +31 (0)20 676 19 18, www.faubourg.nl. The gallery, which is located slightly outside the shopping center but near Vondelpark, offers an interesting selection of contemporary art—not all gay, but much definitely gay inspired. The gallery features everything from ashtrays and paintings to well-crafted statues and body parts, but it's pricey and comparable to vacationing with a rent boy. At least here, you'll find something of lasting value.

GAYS & GADGETS, Nieuwezijds Voorburgwal 110, Tel: +31 (0)20 528 61 87, www.gaysandgadgets.com. An upmarket, bright gay gift shop, G&G is flying the rainbow flag for good reason. This adorable store is stocked with clothing, rainbow stickers, magnets, Oscar Wilde action figures, books, and lubes—really everything from *kunst* (art) to kitsch, depending on personal taste. Peppy background music (Erasure anyone?) and friendly staff keep customers happy, not to mention the reasonable prices on display.

KITSCH KITCHEN, Rozengracht 8-12, Tel: +31 (0)20 428 49 69, www.kitschkitchen.nl. Whoever says Mexican serving trays and Dutch sensibility don't mesh obviously doesn't own this shop. True to its name, this place is overflowing with kitsch, camp, and color—from garish altars and BBQ aprons to plastic mirrors and festive garlands—making it the perfect spot to shop for a Chihuahua's upcoming birthday, if that's what you're in town to do. Products are mostly imported from Mexico.

ODDS & SODS, Eerste Looiersdwarstraat 11, Tel: +31 (0)20 616 84 40, www.odds-sodds.com. For great examples of famous Dutch 20th-century design, Odds & Sods has unbeatable style. The shop specializes in Dutch *jegenstijl,* European art deco, and postmodern design, and offers everything from glass Murano ashtrays and ceramic novelty salad sets to Italian vanity tables. For shoppers who get carried away, this bit of the past might break the bank, but it's hard to resist such a tasteful selection.

TRUELOVE, Prinsenstraat 4, Tel: +31 (0)20 320 25 00, www.truelove.be. How to resist such a name? Crammed into two overstocked, narrow floors brimming with antique bric-a-brac, the store feels like entering a Victorian attic. Amongst faded photographs, paintings, model boats, mink stoles, and old vanity sets, there's hardly space to place your feet, but it's the perfect place for old queens (or those with old money) to shop. Ask in the store for information on their guest house, located just above, or Truelove's apartments in the Jordaan.

Coffee Shops

WHETHER YOU'RE a blunt-smoking pot head, caffeine addict, or just curious, Amsterdam's legendary coffee shops, which are legally licensed to sell pot, are worth checking out. Amsterdam just wouldn't be Amsterdam without it. The city has hundreds of coffee shops, all differing in ambience, quality of weed, and prices, but the less touristy (i.e., outside the Red Light District) the better, especially if you want to avoid Italian teens ditching their school trip.

Unlike rowdier bars, coffee shops are subdued, quiet hangouts. Good coffee shops have a menu, and staff will fully explain each type of weed and its expected effect. Most first-time tourists tend to smoke ganja until they fall over, but it's rarely done by locals.

We're only listing a few shops here, as most will be discovered as you walk around the city. Only the Otherside is exclusively gay.

DAMPRKING, Handboogstraat 29, Tel: +31 (0)20 638 07 05, www.xs4all.nl/~dampweb/. With an extraordinary, fairylike décor that was filmed for a scene in *Ocean's Twelve*, this is one of the city's highly rated coffee shops, especially as far as aesthetics are concerned. The atmosphere is smoky, serene and friendly and while the extensive weed menu leans towards the expensive, the shop has been a consistent winner of the Cannabis Cup. It gets crowded the later it gets, so try to arrive early,

CLUE

Even though it's legal to smoke in coffee shops, attempting to smuggle weed out of Holland is a criminal offense, no matter how insignificant the amount. Try slipping an herbal doggie-bag into your luggage, and a customs officer will put his gloves on in no time. There are far better ways to get a prostate massage.

when you can amble up to the bar proclaiming you'd like a gram of Buddha.

GREENHOUSE, Waterlooplein 345, Tel: +31 (0)20 622 54 99, www.greenhouse.org. If Burt Reynolds and Heather Locklear toking here isn't reason enough to visit, Greenhouse's intimate, small lounge flanked by gold pillars and sunken mosaic stones might be a draw. A *High Times* favorite and frequent Cannabis Cup winner, the coffee shop has a relaxed vibe and while the interior turnstile is initially off-putting, it's actually quite friendly. One of three in the Greenhouse chain, this particular locale is just across from the flea market, and the seating is tight, making it likely that you'll meet your neighbors. There's often strict ID on the door, so be sure to bring a passport.

FAVORITE
COFFEE SHOP NAME

GET A LIFE

THE OTHERSIDE, Regulierdwarsstraat 6, Tel: +31 (0) 20 625 51 41, www.theotherside.nl. What goes together better than hot boys and weed? The Otherside, Amsterdam's sole gay coffee shop, offers joints and cannabis tea—enough to get you and your plaything suitably smashed. While the décor has all the charm of a men's toilet, even with faux chandeliers, the staff is quite friendly and will gladly guide newcomers on how to order bud off the menu. During the warmer months, Queens like to position themselves on the outside benches to spot fresh meat sauntering into the street, though the clientele is usually mixed. Just down the street on the opposite side is coffee shop Betty Too, which isn't gay but boasts a warm, comfortable atmosphere.

DE ROKERIJ III, Amstel 8 +31, Tel: +31 (0)20 620 04 84, www.rokerij.net. A coffee shop with an elaborate, Gothic paint job, the Rokerij on the Amstel is the smallest of the city's four Rokerij coffee shops (which literally means smoking place), all of which are highly popular. This coffee shop is styled after a medieval cathedral, with flickering candles, several winding staircases and enough dark, subdued lighting to make it difficult to leave once you've lit up. Other shops in the chain have Indian and

African motifs and are beautiful places to get buzzed, although the Rokerij's "no hats" policy can irritate those who utilize baseball caps in the same way their grandfathers used comb-overs.

Smart Shops

CONSCIOUS DREAMS, Kokopelli Warmoesstraat 12, Tel: +31 (0)20 421 70 00, www.consciousdreams.nl. When Conscious Dreams became the first shop to sell psychedelic mushrooms over the counter in 1994, the hype guaranteed brisk business. Since then, the shop has expanded to several locations, this one smartly in the Red Light District, and carries everything from magic mushrooms to herbal aphrodisiacs.

Q FACT: George Washington routinely smoked marijuana to relieve pain from rotting teeth. (Remember those wooden choppers?) Washington's own diary recounts his efforts to cultivate and enhance his crops. Under laws written today by U.S. politicians, the first president would have been thrown in prison, guilty of committing a federal felony. Luckily, the same doesn't go for Holland's prime ministry.

Saunas

WITH ITS northern European climate, saunas are popular in Amsterdam and as far as public nudity goes, the Dutch attitude is rather hardnosed: take it off. This pos-

ture equally applies to their windows—shutter- or cur-
tain-less, in a word: exposed—for the Dutch intently believe they've got nothing to hide. "Act normal," goes the
national maxim, "that's already crazy enough." Of course
gay saunas have another purpose entirely, and Amsterdam, though small, boasts one of Europe's largest. Here's
a much-too-short list of the city's gay saunas.

BOOMERANG, Heintjehoeksteeg 8, Tel: +31 (0)20 622 61
62, www.saunaboomerang.nl. The city's most newly-
established gay sauna and situated in the Red Light
District, Boomerang shouldn't be compared to the
larger, well-trafficked Thermos—simply because it
can't compete. Small and intimate, the sauna draws
a different crowd mostly due to its location near the
leather bars, and promotes itself as a leisure club for
gays, bi's, and the curious. So if you're curious, it's
worth checking out. €13.50

THERMOS DAY SAUNA, Raamstraat 33, Tel: +31 (0) 20
623 91 58, www.thermos.nl. A sprawling, five-story
sauna and major tourist attraction, Thermos is the
place for good, clean non-discreet action. The sauna
extends across three buildings, incorporating a steam
bath, sauna, whirlpool, swimming pool, and even a
beauty salon, and offers countless opportunities for
clients to reenact their own version of the film *Some
Like It Hot*. The crowd is mixed, though due to the
influence of free Internet dating, increasingly older
and well-off. While the décor is somewhat dated,
Thermos remains consistently busy, making it the
one place outside the Warmoesstraat where boys
can come to play handball express. One thing to

note before you arrive: The sauna's bizarre policy of supplying one free condom: be prepared and bring your own. €18 (24 and older)

Every first Saturday of the month, the sauna hosts the Dikke Maatjes Sauna for bears, cubs, and their admirers.

THERMOS NIGHT SAUNA, Kerkstraat 58-60, Tel: +31 (0) 20 623 49 36, www.thermos.nl. Yep, Thermos also operates a night venue, though smaller and less extravagant than its day counterpart. Picking up where Thermos Day leaves off, Thermos Night is more matter-of-fact in attitude, as well as décor. The sauna's bar looks right out of Olivia Newton John's video "Physical," (totally appropriate given late-night activities), and draws a younger, cruiser clientele. Multiple entry tickets to both saunas put a nice spin on that hospitality cliché "Come again!" €18 (24 and older)

Saunas for the grrls

EASTERN BATHHOUSE HAMMAM, Zaanstraat 88, Tel: +31 (0)20 681 48 18. For girls who want to keep their knickers on, this traditional woman's *hammam* (that's "bathhouse" in Arabic) is the place to get steamy—if you don't mind bathing with three generations of women. This is like taking a trip to Morocco, no tickets required. €11.00

Public Saunas Frequented by Gay Men and Lesbians

SAUNA DECO, Herengracht 115, Tel: +31 (0)20 623 82 15, www.saunadeco.nl. Flanked by French Art Deco stained-glass and thick, wood walls, Deco houses a

GYMS

CLUE

For those gay gym bunnies who need to flex some muscle, try Splash Health Club (Looiersgracht 26-30 and Lijnbaansgracht 241, www.healthclubsplash.nl), Tijgertje (+31 (0)6 1024 9026, www.tijgertje.ni/index.html) and Barry's Gym (Lijnbaansgracht 350, www.barrysfitness.nl).

gorgeous central lounge, steam baths and a small swimming pool. Not gay but frequented by gay men who simply can't ignore the delicious architecture, Deco is about as close it gets to playing movie starlet out of your own pocket. Unisex, nudity is mandatory, though many clients bring towels. A café, reading tables, and baths are also available. €17

SAUNA FENOMEEN, Eerste Schinkelstraat 14, Tel: +31 (0)20 671 67 80, www.saunafenomeen.nl. Once part of a squat and now legal, this relaxed sauna is a relatively undiscovered spa just south of Vondelpark. Decorated in vivid colors and mosaics, with a solarium and vegetarian cafeteria to boot, it offers a distinct Amsterdam twist on the spa experience. This is an inexpensive escape compared to other venues. €6

Beauty

IT'S A universal truth—one hair salon is as gay as the next—and in Amsterdam, young flirty hairdressers come a dime a dozen. But butch hairdressers are a sight more rare, so we're only listing one. For other hair or waxing needs, there are dozens of salons scattered throughout the city and as easy to find as walking outside your hotel room.

CUTS AND CURLS, Korte Leidsedwarsstraat 75, Tel: +31 (0)20 624 68 81, www.cutsandcurls.com. A small salon with a huge reputation, Cuts and Curls is for walk-ins only. No drive-bys or repeated callbacks accepted—if you want service, you have to prove you want it by coming in and putting your name on the waiting list. A butch hair salon for leather fellas, though ladies, skinheads, and straight boys also wander in, the place has got enough steel siding to make you feel like you've stepped into a shed liquidation sale. With reasonably priced cuts, skirting the range from funky to formal, and friendly, efficient service, being uncut at C&C meets with a totally different reception—like, do you want it shaved or styled?

Sex Shops & Cinemas

ADONIS, Warmoestraat 92, Tel: +31 (0)20 627 29 59, www.
adonis-4men.info. Crowded video/bookshop with
cinema and busy darkroom that will make viewers
lose the plot. Look for Crisco in the window display.

ALFA BLUE, Nieuwendijk 26, Tel: +31 (0)20 627 16 64.
Small but stacked. Gay porn galore.

B1 CINEMA, Regulierbreestraat 4, Tel: +31 (0)20 623 95
46. Not your ordinary sex shop. While the ground
floor offers basic porn fare (DVDs, magazines, sex
toys), go upstairs and you'll find it in action. There
are three floors of porn theaters, the first for heteros,
the top two for gays with a darkroom, lockable
cabins, and glory holes. Curious bi's often meander
up here. Weed smoking prevalent.

BRONX, Kerkstraat 53-55, Tel: +31 (0)20 623 15 48,
www.bronx.nl. Long-running and renovated, this
is the city's largest sex shop. A supermarket for all
your sexual needs, there are more than 40 genres to
choose from, including skinheads, skaters, and foot
fetish. Toys and gifts also available.

DRAKES, Damrak 61, Tel: +31 (0)20 638 23 67, www.
drakes.nl. A well-run, attractive store just off touristy
Damrak, the store offers a range of porn DVDs,
magazines, and toys. Upstairs are cabins for instant
gratification and kids get the breaks: free for under-
20s and half-price for 20–25.

4 MEN, Spuistraat 21, Tel: +31 (0)20 625 87 97, www.
adonis-4men.info. A small cinema, also has private

video room offering tickets that are valid all day. You can flit between 4 Men and its brother organization Adonis.

WILLIAM HIGGINS' LE SALON, Nieuwendijk 20-22, Tel: +31 (0)20 622 65 65. Not sure who Willie is, but the shop sells requisite fare. Small cinema and even smaller video cabins. Many tourists pop in to suddenly discover they're surrounded by gays!

SWEETEN YOUR DAY WITH A STOP AT TAART VAN M'N TANTE.

CHAPTER 5

Dining Out

> The Dutch like dining slowly…so take advantage of the wait by taking in the local eye candy.

WORLD-FAMOUS FOR their chocolate, but definitely *not* their cuisine, the Dutch favor bland meat-and-potatoes fare. They also like a good *worst* or sausage—smoked, boiled, battered, or fried—maybe just a little too much. Traditional staples such as *stampot* (potatoes mashed with vegetables, topped with smoked worst), and the ever-ubiquitous *kroketten* (deep-fried dough, filled with meat or fish) are worth trying. Fortunately, however, Indonesian, Surinamese, Indian, Turkish, Thai, Japanese, Chinese, and European chow tip the balance, offering tourists more choice than just *broodjes* (sandwiches) with cheese. If you're daring, there's always herring (or *haring)*, a local staple sold at canal-side kiosks. Below, our list of gay and mixed venues to satisfy your palette while swilling the local brew or alternatively, intoxicating the local swine.

BACKSTAGE, Utrechtsedwarsstraat 67, Tel: +31 (0)20 622 36 38. At Backstage, a café/knitwear boutique/ hangout owned by Gary, the living half of the Christmas Twins (his brother and fellow cabaret performer Greg died years ago), everyone knows your name. For tourists traipsing in, it's a bit of a throwback, but stick around long enough and 70-something Gary is likely to approach asking, "What's your sign, honey?" et voila, an instant karma reading. For a taste of real Amsterdam (circa 1970s–1980s) hosted by an African-American who used to headline the European nightclub circuit, this is the place to grab a coffee.

CAFÉ DE JAREN, Nieuwe Doelenstraat 20, Tel: +31 (0)20 625 57 71, www.cafe-de-jaren.nl. Not specifically gay, Café de Jaren is one of the city's largest cafés and draws attractive crowds—gay? you'll have to guess—who like to see and be seen, especially on its picturesque back terrace (which you'll have to jockey for to find a seat). On the ground floor, it's a vast, cavernous café and reading room and on the second, a restaurant. Soup, sandwiches, and overworked waiters are standard fare, but it's the congenial atmosphere that packs crowds in—that or entirely reasonable prices.

DOLORES, Nieuwezijds Voorburgwal (opposite 289), Tel: +31 (0)20 620 33 02. An organic snack bar crammed into a converted tram shed (which is an 1896 monument), Dolores serves a variety of organic fare, veggie burgers, coffees, juices, and other healthy, reasonably-priced snacks. Always busy, it's a great spot for wholesome midnight belly busters, too. In the winter, the funky if claustrophobic interior draws health junkies who don't mind eating within an elbow's distance. During summer, outdoor tables offer a perfect view of the tram tracks, tourists, and cyclists attempting to ride over both.

DOWNTOWN, Reguliersdwarsstraat 31, Tel: +31 (0)20 622 99 58, www.coffeeshopdowntown.nl. Touting itself *the* day time meeting place for gays and lesbians, Downtown actually has good reason. Open since 1970, the tiny café pulls in diverse crowds because Fokke and Frits (both founders, not menu items) insisted on curtainless windows and keeping everything out in the open. A basic menu, including toasted sandwiches, offers simple, inexpensive fare but this place is definitely not for the claustrophobic. There are usually too many guys, tired from shopping, resting here to guarantee ample leg room. If you prefer something that's not on the menu, accommodation is also available upstairs—so ask at the café.

GARLIC QUEEN, Reguliersdwarsstraat 27, Tel: +31 (0)20 422 64 26, www.garlicqueen.nl. Yes, it's garlic galore! Every single entry, including dessert, is made with garlic (the "stewed beef" tops 60 cloves) making this *not* the place to bring a date for your first kiss. Between the garlic and portraits of Queen Beatrix, you'll be able to brag—from a safe distance—to friends that you've had a new dining experience. Great dishes include Garlic Baker, an elephant head of garlic baked in a ceramic dish with olive

CLUE

The Dutch like dining slowly and their service reflects it. Between ordering from less-than-attentive waiters and finally getting the bill, even having a sandwich could take two hours, so take advantage of the wait by taking in the local eye candy.

oil and herbs, which is spread on homemade bread. Reservations are recommended as the restaurant is rather small.

GETTO, Warmoesstraat 51, Tel: +31 (0)20 421 51 51, www.getto.nl. Trendy yet unpretentious, Getto attracts boys and girls and offers a lively camp ambience alongside home-style dishes. The mixed international crowd ranges from beautiful boys and their admirers to dressed-down tourists eager to schmooze, booze, and later, cruise. The menu offers everything from juicy burgers to African vegetarian pancakes, and every Wednesday is Burger Queens night, with patties at reduced prices. Just don't forget to order home fries for your home boy—or he might pout during the wait. Tuesday night is reserved for lesbians.

GRAND CAFÉ RESTAURANT 1ST CLASS, Centraal Station Spoor 2B, Tel: +31 (0)20 625 01 31, www.restauranteersteklas.nl. Often overlooked by tourists, Centraal Station's Grand Café, is an ideal meeting place with fine food and an atmosphere that harks back to the 1880s. If you're looking to escape the hustle between tracks, the restaurant is a beautiful oasis with large windows, mirrors, and porcelain vases. An excellent French menu with moderate prices keeps Dutch customers, who are notorious penny-pinchers, satisfied. Worth a look for dedicated dandies.

HEMELSE MODDER, Oude Waal 9, Tel: +31 (0)20 624 32 03, www.hemelsemodder.nl. With well-spaced tables and an elegant, if minimalist décor (think Ikea-inspired with darker hues), the restaurant focuses its creativity on its menu. From lamb's steak with pistachio tapenade crust, to vegetarian herb pancakes, the food always delivers—one of the main reasons why this gay dining hot spot continually draws mainstream crowds. Its three best advantages: a beautiful location on one of the city's widest canals; flirty, helpful waiters; and a menu that has met with ongoing success, like the restaurant's namesake dessert, the Hemelse Modder, or heavenly mud, a mountain of a devilishly crafted mousse.

KITSCH, Utrechtsestraat 42, Tel: +31 (0)20 625 92 51, www.restaurant-kitsch.nl. Kitsch is where fine dining meets informal. For the ambience, think eclectic—neon, retro '70s décor mixed with aerobic videos from the '80s, and *Starsky and Hutch* photos lining the walls. The multi-level restaurant, which leaves space for groups as well as couples, offers a menu that varies from lobster thermidor to juicy Kitsch burgers and a wine list featuring the Betty Ford Clinic logo, making a good fit for every type of wallet, personality, or dysfunction. Also, the "kitschen"

DUTCH DELIGHTS

JAPANESE PANCAKE WORLD, Tweede Egelantiersdwarsstraat 24a, Tel: +31 (0)20 320 44 47, www.japanesepancakeworld.com. It's no surprise Europe's only Japanese pancake house would set up digs here, where pancakes are a beloved national dish. Slightly stodgier than typical Dutch fare and with a delicious Asian twist, savory Japanese-style *Okonomi* will set your wallet back €8–€9 and your stomach a good half day. Not a queer venue, this restaurant draws clientele who know a good "cheese Osaka" when they see one. A great date place because the ordering is simple—leaving you ample time to focus on his eyes…

is open till late, so you can enjoy a late night meal before hitting gay hotspots on Regulierdwarsstraat. If you're a gal, persuade your date to order more "pussy and potatoes," which means oysters with French fries to the folks around here.

MANKIND, Weteringstraat 60, Tel:+31 (0)20 638 47 55, www.mankind.nl. Friendly, but nondescript, this café overlooks the quiet Lijnbaansgracht canal, which is close to the Rijksmuseum. Relaxing and tucked nicely away on a small street, the café offers good food and plenty of gay maps/information.

ME NAAM NAAM, Koningsstraat 29, Tel: +31 (0)20 423 33 44, www.menaamnaam.nl. If you've never been to

Bangkok, Me Naam Naam's perfect for taking a quick culinary tour. Thai standards like Pad Thai and Tom Yam soup and an array of traditional curries pack the crowds in quickly, so best to reserve first. If the food's not enough, waiter Saskin dresses in traditional Thai clothing that's about as camp and colorful as anything you'd find in Rodgers and Hammerstein's *The King and I*. The restaurant is located near the Red Light District and offers superb food.

PANNENKOEKEN HUIS UPSTAIRS, Grimburgwal 2, Tel: +31 (0)20 626 56 03. If you've summed up enough Dutch courage to try Dutch food, this is the place to do it. A steep climb up an impossibly narrow staircase, this miniscule restaurant lies around the corner from the University of Amsterdam, and is lost in time (as are most traditionally Dutch venues). Here you'll find pictures of the royal family (also yellowed and outdated), ceramic teapots dangling overhead, and the cook—who also doubles as waiter, dishwasher, and management—making pancakes with two gas cookers. But Dutch pancakes, more like crepes than their thicker American counterparts, are fantastic and rarely fail to impress tourists. Reservations recommended as the restaurant seats about a dozen.

LE MONDE, Rembrandtplein 6, Tel: +31 (0)20 626 99 22. A favorite of gay tourists, locals, and straights who pool on the café terrace unaware of their queer surroundings, Le Monde offers Brazilian-Dutch food, a seeming culinary oxymoron. The restaurant's best feature is the outdoor terrace on Rembrandtplein, a popular, crowded tourist destination during the summer and great for people watching, especially if you're a straight guy searching for your lost Lolita. Aside from voyeuristic opportunities, the food is good and prices reasonable.

MOEDERS, Rozengracht 251, Tel: +31 (0)20 626 79 57, www.moeders.com. A boon to mothers everywhere, the restaurant uses both traditional Dutch and international recipes, all by actual mothers god bless 'em, to create their menu. Warmly decorated, just as you'd expect Mom's house to be, it offers real comfort food like ribs, hashed meat, and Dutch *stampot*, a stodgy concoction of mashed vegetables with a thick worst on top. For Mama's boys, this is definitely the place to dine—the interior walls are crowded with pictures of mothers and you're even encouraged to bring your own (picture, or the real thing).

NO NAME, Wolvenstraat 23, Tel: +31 (0)20 320 08 43. What's in a name? Nothing, really, if this well-run, sleek restaurant, which has built its reputation on efficient service, has anything to say about it. Hip, relaxed, and bathed in neutral tones, the place resembles an upscale hair salon with glossy fashion magazines scattered throughout, chatty clientele, and changing art exhibitions on the wall. On the menu are delicious Asian salads, dim sum, sizeable sandwiches, and if you sit next to the bar, cocktails galore.

THE OLD HIGHLANDER, St. Jacobsstraat 8, Tel: +31 (0)20 420 83 21. Amsterdam's sole Scottish eatery with a menu as wide as a wind-blown kilt, the restaurant serves up portions hearty enough to fuel a leather all-nighter. Whether it's steak for breakfast, baked beans, or an omelet washed down with a glass of

CHOLESTEROL CLOGGERS

REMEMBER JOHN TRAVOLTA'S *Pulp Fiction* line about how the Dutch eat French fries with mayonnaise? ("I seen 'em do it, man. They fuckin' drown 'em in that shit.") It's true—and delicious. If the urge hits to do the same, here's an ordering guide. Fries with mayo is called *patat met*; fries with mayo, ketchup, and onions is called *patat speciaal,* and for a gut buster, *patat speciaal* plus peanut satay sauce equals *patat oorlog* (translation: "war fries," so don't wear Van Ravenstein while eating it or you may have to enter into battle with your drycleaner).

wine, the menu is as flexible as your morals after a dozen drinks. Waterfalls and bridges add to the eclectic décor and once you've washed it all down, step next door to the Web, which shares the same owner, to parade your bulging...stomach?

PALEIS VAN DE WEEMOED, Oudezijds Voorburgwal 15, Tel: +31 (0)20 625 69 64, www.paleis-van-de-weemoed.nl. Amsterdam's answer to Moulin Rouge, this intimate restaurant/theater offers camp, colorful cabaret, and a four-course French meal that gives its working-class sister *'t Sluisje* a run for the money. A mix of drag queens, live performances, nostalgic music and imaginative entertainment, the theater packs mostly straight guests but the program appeals to any gay music aficionado with a taste for red plush curtains, flamboyant artists, and great cuisine.

REIBACH, Sarphatistraat 45, Tel: +31 (0)20 626 77 08, www.reibach.nl. While the restaurant changed its location off one of Amsterdam's most beautiful canals to a larger, more remote (if you're a tourist) spot, it still offers good ol' queer hospitality. The café is clean, spacious, with clear plastic chairs, and possesses that kind of Dutch designer chic that some find too minimalist, but the cute waiter adds much to the décor. The menu's good, with a nice selection of sandwiches, soup, and even crème brulee but the café's best feature is service with a smile—which you will learn is about as common as a hit single by Deee-Lite.

'T SLUISJE, Torensteeg 1, Tel: +31 (0)20 624 08 13, www.sluisje.nl. If you're looking for camp cabaret to go with your wiener schnitzel, this is the place—granted there's seating available. A popular venue for bachelorette parties, dyke get-togethers, and gay family outings, the restaurant is always booked weekends, so reservations are absolutely recommended. While hearty food, attentive waiters, and a drag show featuring standard lip-syncing divas are the biggest draw (but for non-Dutch speaking customers, much of the charm is lost), the audience is equally worth watching for its spontaneous, drunken outbreaks. If you're looking for cozy, crowded, and thoroughly Dutch in its most provincial way, this is the venue. If you actually want a place to sit, however, across the street there's Franken & Kok—a stylish venue that by name alone should be gay.

SATURNINO, Reguliersdwarsstrat 5, Tel: +31 (0)20 639 01 02. Thanks to good prices, quality food, friendly service, and a delightful atmosphere, this bustling bistro has to be Italian. Not gay, an exception on terribly gay Regulierdwarsstraat, the place scores high with pasta lovers who bellow for tables in one of its three art deco dining rooms. When it comes to the menu, it's the usual suspects—pizza, pasta, and flirty waiters, though sadly, they're probably straight.

SMALL WORLD, Binnen Oranjestraat 14, Tel: +31 (0)20 420 27 74. For down under hospitality, this busy corner café run by a friendly gay Aussie and his equally sociable staff serves up delicious sandwiches with atypically efficient service. There's a great selection of sandwiches, breads, creamy pasta salads, and even Aussie meat pie, a rare find outside the island, and while slightly pricey (though not for this part of town), the portions are filling. The café faces coffee shop Relax, which is appropriate given Small World's casual ambience.

LA STRADA, Nieuwezijds Voorburgwal 93, Tel: +31 (0)20 625 02 76. Located away from the Red Light District, this is a place where working girls—lesbians, that is— like to rest their feet. The bar-restaurant, built into two adjacent houses, has a spacious, warmly decorated interior with plentiful flowers, a huge "La Strada" poster and a decent Euro (French-Italian-Spanish) menu that pulls in mixed crowds. Friendly service, a rare find in Amsterdam, ultra-reasonable prices, and queer sensibility don't hurt either.

SUPPERCLUB, Jonge Roelensteeg 21, Tel: +31 (0)20 344 64

00, www.supperclub.nl. Supperclub has been a magnet for well-heeled visitors since its opening. Trendy to the point of being passé, the restaurant-bar-performance-space, holds 130 diners a night and dinner runs €65 for a five-course meal served in bed—or dripped over guests, according to the waiter's whim. An all-night experience, dining here is somewhat of an interactive performance, with VJs, DJs, and wily waiters vying for your attention, bullying you to sip your Barolo or cuddling up for a chat between courses. While the food includes delightful combinations, Supperclub is less of a restaurant and more of a portal to another galaxy. Gay or straight toilets and a reputation for kink are also a big draw. Reservations here are highly advised and don't forget to bring your mortgage papers—you might need them to fund a round of aperitifs. Also check out their Supperclub Cruise, the Supperclub on water.

DE TAART VAN M'N TANTE, Ferdinand Bolstraat 10, Tel: +31 (0)20 776 46 00, www.detaart.com. Meaning "my auntie's tart/cake"—not "my aunt is a tart"—this kitsch café puts liberal icing on its stylishly high-profile cakes. Owners Seimon and Noam, graduating from making edible clothing to cakes that cameo in award-winning films, have created several-tiered culinary sensations that keep customers salivating. Their tea house (located below the duo's B&B *Cake Under My Pillow*) is full of locals eagerly sinking their teeth into superbly saccharine delights. The neon pink, Barbie's playhouse-inspired décor attracts kiddies, too, and those aiming for a swift sugar high.

URBAN PICNIC, Oude Spiegelstraat 4, Tel: +31 (0)20 320 88 66, www.urbanpicnic.net. Offering a healthy selection of organic teas, juices, and vegetarian food while showcasing contemporary and vintage Dutch furniture, this café puts the spotlight on good taste. Dine on goat cheese sandwiches amongst cupboards, armoires, and funky tableware. Shoppers are encouraged to buy it if they like it—including the chairs they're sitting on. If you like reading interior design magazines while daydreaming about what to buy next, this is the spot for you.

THE COCKRING: THERE'S ALWAYS ENTRY.

CHAPTER 6

The Bar Scene

The Reguliersdwarsstraat is
happy-hour heaven.

AMSTERDAM IS the place to abandon inhibitions
so how better to do it than boozing? That's what
the locals do. Mere centuries back, the city's canals
were so filthy that drinking water actually had to be
shipped in, and beer, considered both cheaper and
safer to drink, became the daily standard. Today the
city boasts a dizzying array of watering holes, with
gay bars prominently in the mix. There are leather
bars, yuppie bars, neighborhood bars with local
flavor, lesbian bars, hustler bars, fetish bars, and chic
designer bars—enough choice to keep your mind
muddled, never mind the rounds at happy hour. To
further dampen your chances of sobriety, gay venues
tend to clutter together (leather bars crowd the leather
street, camp bars another), making bar hopping in
Amsterdam, which is already extremely compact,
hopelessly easy.

Before choosing an outfit and rushing out, it's useful
to get your bearings first. While there's no true gay

ghetto in Amsterdam, gay bars can be found in three predominant areas.

> For an underrated brown café environment, head for bars along the Amstel River, where locals are ready to croon Robbie Williams interspersed with Dutch folk tunes—yep, that camp '70s aura still holds sway.
>
> Worth noting, the Kerkstraat, one of the city's oldest gay areas, has ebbed over the years into a handful of hotels and porn shops. Aside from the Spijker bar, your drinking options are elsewhere.
>
> For Dolce & Gabbana–clad boys seeking the lounge world of high alcohol and high design, the Reguliersdwarsstraat is happy hour heaven. Here you'll find trendy bars continually opening and closing for an even trendier overhaul, and an energetic pre-clubbing scene. This is the most vanilla part of town.
>
> And finally, in the Red Light District along the Warmoesstraat, one of Amsterdam's oldest streets and a former Mecca for lodging sailors, are the leather bars, such as Argos, Cockring, and Dirty Dicks, running the A to Zs in sleaze.

We've organized bars according to area, but if you tire of one, the others are within walking distance. Lesbian bars are listed separately, though the city's gay bars, aside from the few billed as men only, are far from exclusive—open to anyone ready to part with a few Euros.

THE ROUTINE

AMSTERDAM'S GAYS follow a specific drill when it comes to bar hopping. Get the routine wrong, and you'll be convinced either the city's deserted or the local tourist office has hatched a sinister ploy to pull gay dollars without putting out. Generally speaking, the gay community goes out late (primping and preening takes time) and 11 p.m. is a good time to start.

So here's the schedule:

NEAR THE AMSTEL, locals flit between Montmartre, which throbs with activity during happy hours 6–8, and Mix, finally ending up in Entre Nous.

ALONG TRENDY REGULIERSDWARSSTRAAT, April's happy hour runs first from 6 to 7, Monday to Friday, followed by Soho's at midnight. On weekends, many drinkers continue at neighboring Exit to dance.

IN THE LEATHER BELT, the Cuckoo's Nest and the Web start early, followed by the Argos. After midnight, patrons filter into the Eagle, later followed by the Cockring for dancing or Dirty Dicks, which is self-explanatory.

Lesbian Bars

IN DIRECT contrast to the city's abundance of gay venues, the lesbian scene is minuscule (but this goes without saying for most major capitals). There are only five women's bars and a handful of one-off women's parties at scattered venues, leaving ladies few cruising options or requiring the stealth of a private eye to track down women-only events. To be fair, Amsterdam is small, making its dyke bar quotient reasonable.

CUSTOM CAFÉ SUGAR, Hazenstraat 19, Tel: + 31 (0)6 140 131 43, www.les-bi-friends.com. Amsterdam's most modern lesbian bar (though it touts itself as also bi and gay) Sugar has given a fresh thrust to a scene that's all but lost its momentum. Established by young dykes who wanted to take matters into their own hands, the bar, which is aimed at a younger demographic, helps fill a yawning gap in the lesbian scene—if you can call it that—which tends towards an older clientele. A cool, arty dive with colorful pillows, lots of mirrors, and a healthy contingent of committed regulars (a plus, given its recent entry on the scene), Sugar is buzzing with social activity. So much so, it has become a local media darling—which probably says more about the local mainstream media (ohmigod, a *lesbian* bar? Cover it!) than the bar itself, whose owners are ambitious in promoting estrogen pursuits.

BROWN CAFÉS

OLD STYLE, traditional Dutch cafés, so-called from years—centuries, in some cases—of tobacco smoke that has darkened and stained the walls, *bruin cafés* or *bruine kroeg* are dusky, unpretentious watering holes often serving nothing but standard pilsner. Even for non-beer lovers who prefer high-octane cocktails, it's worth a visit for a glimpse of everyday city life.

SAAREIN II, Elandstraat 119, Tel: +31 (0)20 623 49 01. One of Amsterdam's most long-established lesbian bars with a loyal feminist following, Saarein has a true *gezellig*—the Dutch concept of cozy—brown-bar (i.e., traditional—see sidebar above) atmosphere. The bar opened as a political café in the late '70s and still retains some of the decade's character, but men are now allowed, and the bar holds a monthly transgender café every third Monday of the month. Split into several levels, the attractive interior dates back to the 19th century, and is a mellow place to grab a slow drink or shoot a game of pool downstairs. Saarein offers bingo nights, pub quizzes, and sing-along evenings (with lyrics supplied) every second Sunday.

VIVELAVIE, Amstelstraat 7, Tel: +31 (0)20 624 01 14, www.vivelavie.net. This smart, well-known, busy bar is home to chic lesbians in their mid-20s to 30s and their male friends, when accompanied. While some nights are s-l-o-w, others are as crowded as a packed subway during rush hour, but regardless, the music's loud enough to rival a marching band and luckily, it's not all Shakira (though many ladies would do her if she sidled up to the bar). Parties are held throughout the year, allowing girls to get their freak on while fighting the stereotype that once lesbians settle, their only interests are getting a cat, gaining considerable weight, and never leaving home again.

YOU II, Amstel 178, www.youii.nl, Tel: +31 (0)20 420 43 11. Home to a similar crowd as Vivelavie, which lies just around the corner, You II attracts baby dykes hunting for late-night drinks accompanied by their equally juvenile male friends, rent boys, women in their 30s, and the occasional, inevitable late-night dyke brawl. More dance club than watering hole, with a stylish, lengthy stained glass light hovering over the bar and plentiful mirrors, the bar has tried to fill a gap in Amsterdam's otherwise comprehensive gay club scene. While the music is good enough to rival larger clubs, the bar doesn't always attract hordes—it really depends on the night and the hour. But the "fish market" (that's meat market with a twist!) predictably thrives the later it gets.

CAFÉ SAPPHO, Wijzelstraat 103, www.sapho.nl. Sappho, which touts itself as a "multicultural, multisexual and multiartistic bar," is an artsy, atmospheric watering hole offering something for everyone—though by name alone, it should solely be reserved for lesbians. Friday nights there's Female Sensual, a full-out estrogen affair that can get packed (and it's free); Saturdays are reserved for mixed nights and DJ parties, and weekdays live performances, expositions, theater, and film take center stage. After facing pending bankruptcy and temporarily closing shop, Sappho managed to bounce back beautifully, proving girls won't always take it lying down. Good news, too, because the bar's always a friendly place.

Tranny Bars

UNLIKE LARGER metropolises, Amsterdam's transvestite scene is minuscule, leaving those who like drag fewer options than shoe stores normally provide. To make matters worse, the local community tends to throw transvestites and transsexuals in the same pot, though not all chicks with dicks are of the same feather. Transgender get-togethers happen monthly at Saarein II (see p. 111) but for pure Dutch drag (which is frumpier than you'd expect) the following are the places to go:

LELLEBEL, Utrechtsestraat 4, Tel: +31 (0)20 427 51 39, www.lellebel.nl. A tiny, popular drag bar just off Rembrandtplein, Lellebele, which translates as "floozy," is pure entertainment. Akin to finding yourself in a cheap '70s wedding reception held in someone's uncle's garage, the narrow bar welcomes transvestites and transsexuals (though most of them seem to be behind the bar or working the mike) and a loyal local following. On various nights there's live cabaret, karaoke, salsa parties, an open podium, and the occasional spontaneous multilingual bitchfest—just another highly anticipated form of diversion. A great place for late night drinks, inappropriate behavior and off-key (or off-color) show tunes, Lellebel might prove a challenge to stray hetero men who, if they've ever heard a Lou Reed lyric, know too many drinks leads to a walk on the wild side—though Dutch drag is somewhat dated, greatly reducing the risk.

QUEEN'S HEAD, Zeedijk 20, Tel: +31 (0)20 420 24 75, www.queenshead.nl. Once an Amsterdam institution (due to former drag host Dusty), the Queen's Head is less camp and kitsch than in its heyday, but has remained a decidedly unpretentious, welcoming place. The dimly-lit bar, which displays a line of butch Ken dolls in its front window, attracts older men, skinheads, Brits, tourists, and regulars who come for a friendly drink or to take in the occasional cabaret with Dutch lip-syncing divas (whose best number has to be "Your Son Will Come Out Tomorrow," based on *Annie*). By the toilet downstairs there's a remarkable canal view, perfect for a romantic make-out session if you don't mind the anatomically correct Barbies housed in glass cases overhead, watching your particular brand of lip syncing.

The Amstel

FULL OF traditional bars and loyal locals, this is the authentic, camp Dutch experience.

DE AMSTEL TAVEERNE, Amstel 54, Tel. +31 (0)20 623 42 54. As Dutch as Edam, the Amstel is one of the area's longest-standing gay bars and dishes out plenty of cheese of its own. The spacious bar attracts large, friendly crowds who burst into sing-a-longs, and offers traditional (read: kitsch) Dutch ambience—beer mugs hanging from rafters over the bar, Delft tiles, and decades-old faded photos of former patrons stuck to the back walls. On warm summer nights the mixed, 30s-on-up crowd spills out onto the street facing the river and on colder ones, the regulars (mostly flannel fellows) enjoy talking to their husbands about what to buy next at Ikea. This is a real Dutch experience.

THE BOYS, Amstel 140. Open weekends only, this is a small after-hours club for partiers, rent boys, insomniacs, and stray cats.

CÁFE ROUGE, Amstel 60, Tel. +31 (0)20 420 98 81, www.caferouge.nl. Café Rouge is a slightly upmarket old-fashioned *gezellig* bar crammed with queens—or really, their portraits. The kitsch red velvet interior boasts pictures of queens, princesses, members of the royal family (who're definitely queer, depending on how you define it), and the greatest queen of all time, Mother Virgin Mary. The bar is dominated by disco balls, chandeliers, enormous bouquets of red roses, and oversized gilt frames, but the patrons are much less camp than those you'll find at Montmartre around the corner. A welcoming, popular place, it gets packed late, drawing much of the Amstel Taveenne's clientele.

ENTRE NOUS, Halvemaansteeg 14, Tel. +31 (0)20 623 17 00. This bar is popular late-late night when other bars have closed and as a result, packed to its tiny little rim. The '80s will never, ever die here, and Eurovision is another must. The clientele is friendly, a mix of young and old, those wanting to keep that night torch alive, and Amsterdam's hard-living girls.

HOTSPOT, Amstel 102, Tel: +31 (0)20 622 83 35. While most of the customers here look like they were born when Kylie Minogue was still acting in *Neighbors*, the bar has its pluses—like a big video screen at the back and sleek seating. That aside, it's small, chic, unassuming, and best to visit after the clock strikes 12.

DE KROKODIL, Amstelstraat 34, Tel: +31 (0)20 626 22 43. A bar for really old guys, the Krokodil's not afraid to tout its old-fashioned interior, nor its graying clientele. The bar, which boasts the same owner for the last 25 years, looks like a bar, with nothing distinct save a poster of a crocodile. But it's friendly—just like you'd expect old-timers to be—and especially packed on Sunday afternoons during happy hour.

MIX CAFÉ, Amstel 50, Tel: +31 (0)20 420 33 88, www.mixcafe.nl. Mix is aptly named, drawing a crowd of gays, lesbians, straight women, and the occasional straight man (or is he just a lost tourist)? The youngish crowd blends in with the bar's aged striped wallpaper, which is reminiscent of Dutch grand cafés, though here much less gaudy. While regulars like to keep to themselves, the atmosphere is relaxed enough. The music is loud and a solid mix of '70s Dutch pop, obscure German disco, ABBA, and other numbers that will catapult you straight back to those days of bad highlights and even worse perms. There's the odd karaoke night but the bar is far from camp. This is a good place to have a drink before moving on to bigger, or bawdier, venues.

MONTMARTRE, Halvemaansteeg 17 Tel: +31 (0)20 620 76 22. A fun, festive, and popular little brother to nearby Amstel Taveerne, this bar attracts a mixed crowd of cute boys and girls, from fresh young colts to matured daddies, ready to dance the second a drink enters their hands. Styled as a mock French café, though it could easily pass as something Las Vegas, the bar has—or actually *is*—a small, well-trodden dance floor and the music ventures from camp, Dutch chart standards (yes, cheese is borderless) and golden oldies to sugary Eurovision hits. Weekends and happy hours pull in H&M victims and fashionable dykes whose sole purpose is to sweat and flirt. Consistently voted Amsterdam's best gay bar, Montmartre will soon host its own reality TV soap opera series (as if gay life ain't soap opera enough) where viewers can follow the extraordinary goings on of its fabulous staff. How absolutely nosey!

HET WAPEN VAN LONDEN, Amstel 14, Tel: +31 (0)6 153 953 17, www.wapenvanlonden.nl. Run by the former owner of hustler bar the Music Box, who hooked up with a Czech and decided to go British, Het Wapen looks like a throw back from Maggie Thatcher's reign. Busy early evening, with a mixed crowd (locals, Czechs, gays, including transsexuals, straights, and street boys), the bar is decorated like an English university bar from the '80s—with the music, to boot. Like many local watering holes that have the habit of putting every single glass they own on the bar, Het Wapen is no exception. But somehow, while the décor lacks sophistication, this is a terribly relaxed place.

DUTCH DRINKING PRACTICES

IF YOU never let the words "no head" escape your lips, Dutch bars might prove an exception. Order a beer and you'll get a two-finger thick head of foam—a tradition locals say guarantees clean ale, but sounds more like a justification for being expertly fleeced. Dare to comment, and the bartender will deliver a look of haughty disdain, mouthing the word "foreigner" in a minimum of four languages under his breath.

When it comes to actually getting rid of your beer, you'll also get a sour deal. Most venues charge .50 cents for the pleasure of release (i.e., using the bathroom) and frequent trips don't lead to discounts. Try to sneak past, and who-ever's watching guard will remind you of your financial duties. The Dutch are so frugal with cash, even Benjamin Franklin (who admittedly, never used a gay toilet) commented centuries ago: The thrifty maxim of the wary Dutch/Is to save all the Money they can touch.

Not on the Amstel, but Traditional

CAFÉ DE BARDERIJ, Zeedijk 14, tel: +31 (0)20 420 51 32.
A traditional brown café (an old-style café, so-called from years—centuries, in some cases—of tobacco

smoke that has darkened the walls) with a mixed, middle-aged clientele, this place probably checks ID on the door—born after 1965? No entry! Or maybe it's the loud Dutch accordion sing-a-longs that send pectoral beefcake scampering. Still, the place is friendly, with a romantic view of several canals, a tickle room (thought to be where prostitutes played with clients) and downstairs, there's a darkish basement where Netherbears are known to occasionally lurk. The only babes you'll find here are boomers.

Regulierdwarsstraat

THE NEIGHBORHOOD where air kisses abound, a.k.a. vanilla central and a first stop for gay tourists.

APRIL, Reguliersdwarsstraat 37, Tel: +31 (0)20 625 95 72. A large, modern cocktail lounge where leather-scene and fashion queens mix, April is busy weekends and absolutely packed to its gills on Sunday during 2-for-1 happy hours. A revolving floor out back with several video screens behind it is the bar's coolest feature, but no Dramamine needed as rough estimates clock it at twenty minutes per revolution. While neighboring bar Soho has upstaged April, making it a bit past its prime, it's much easier to grab a front table here and watch the gay Cinderella world traipse by—especially as the bar is quite deserted outside happy hour. This is a good first stop for tourists.

ARC, Reguliersdwarstraat 44, Tel: +31 (0)20 689 70 70, www.bararc.com. Trendy, modern, well-designed and the place to be if you're young, good-looking

DRINK SPECIALS

WEED ASIDE, Amsterdam's best incentive to have a good time is happy hour—or, more appropriately, *hours.* Unlike bars in the United States, which offer discounts at the same time, gay Dutch bars have coordinated and staggered their happy hours, stretching 2-for-1 drinks well into the night. The philosophy: Why compete for the same men when you can please 'em all in stages? Also, don't expect several drinks for half the price, because when it comes to drinking, the Dutch are severely pragmatic. Order two beers and the bartender will hand you four—there's no time to waste when the bar's full.

5–7 p.m. Getto's happy hour (Warmoesstraat), 6–7 p.m. April (Regulierdwarsstraat), 6–8 p.m. Montmartre (off the Amstel) 12–1 a.m. Soho (Reuglierdwarsstraat)

and like to be ignored, Arc resembles a flashy, though relaxed New York bar. Pretentious and overcrowded because there's nowhere else as pretentious and overcrowded in the city, the bar was remodeled into a bar/restaurant, but the bar ultimately won so cocktails flow easily, rarely impeded by finger food. A mixed crowd usually lounges into the early hours and the bar's cocktails are definitely addictive. While the see-me queens might come for the mirrored men's toilets, most clientele seem to enjoy bathing in its swish and swank, purple hued interior—a reflection of their true Calvin Klein inner selves.

LUST FOR LEKKER

The word *lekker* is usually one of the first Dutch words foreigners pick up—one, because it's repeated ad infinitum and two, to the untrained ear, it sounds a bit like "liquor." Meaning? There are many: great, attractive, cool, pleasant, enjoyable, nice, anything considered marginally above average, and frequently, delicious. Applied to the physical world, *lekker* focuses on the idea of tastiness, such as *lekker eten* (great food), *lekker ding* (nice piece of ass), or *lekkere stoot,* (a hot chick/hunk, and something you'd like to—or already have—sampled).

SOHO, Reguliersdwarsstraat 36, Tel: +31 (0)20 422 33 12. A gay English pub situated firmly in Amsterdam, Soho just broadens the city's queerness. While a bar that's two-stories large, with exaggerated Victorian décor, plush leather chairs, and faux yellowed ceilings might not sound like the "It" place to be, Soho crowds quickly, especially when happy hour kicks off at midnight. Cruisy, though overly willing young boys are most likely rent boys, the bar has a healthy following of yuppies and other cinderfellas who like to soak up its tasteful masculine atmosphere. The toilet, up a narrow set of wooden stairs, might prove a challenge to wobbly, beer-saturated knees, but if you dash for a slash outside, you could be fined. All in all, this is a highly popular bar and for good reason.

Eduardo of the Argos

WHAT'S IT LIKE owning the famed Argos? Says Brazilian Eduardo Bettega Curial, its proprietor for twelve years, "The bar's given me the opportunity to do what I like—to talk and make friends." But conversation isn't why his customers flock here. Since its establishment in 1953, the Argos has laid claim to Amsterdam's first darkroom and steady, repeat business ever since. "Monday to Monday, there's always someone to do," says Curial. "Downstairs [in the darkroom] there's no talk, it's just action."

Before taking over the Argos, Curial was former assistant director of gay nights at the RoXY, Amsterdam's most famed disco during the '90s, which suffered a fire in 1999 that closed the place indefinitely. Renowned for creating outrageous, lewd, and shocking stage acts (like onstage paint enemas or power drilling a dildo into a participant), Curial moved on when the bar became available. "It was one of the first bars I went to in Amsterdam and it soon became my favorite place," he says, though initially, even Curial wasn't comfortable with the leather scene. "I didn't really have a gay life in Brazil, so I found the serious, ultra-masculine aesthetic intimidating."

But obviously not today and the Argos's ongoing popularity, particularly due to its darkroom, is constant proof. According to Curial, the bar has attracted its fair share of celebrities, and eccentric fetishists, but mostly men with one thing on their minds. "The Argos is the place to fuck and go," he says. But sometimes, customers have been too fast to exit, leaving their toys behind. Curial has discovered everything from lost cockrings, dildos, salted cucumbers, and trousers ("I really don't know how they go home without them,") to a set of dentures, which the customer later retrieved. "We don't ask. Who am I to judge?" he laughs.

Warmoestraat

THE LEATHER belt, where you'll find boys in rawhide grazing through the fetish fields.

ARGOS, Warmoesstraat 95, Tel. +31 (0)20 622 65 95, www.argosbar.com. A straight-forward, means-business leather bar, Argos is supposedly the city's oldest and definitely, its most iconic. Strictly men only, the bar is considered a leather man's dream for a basement darkroom that's as high on action as it is low on wattage. Upstairs, you'll find the requisite bulky ship chains and hooks, dusty, weathered lamps and thick wooden floors that appeal to the ultra masculine, not to mention porn videos that rouse the teasing and greasing that goes on downstairs. Owner and doorman Eduardo, a friendly, towering Brazilian, ensures the masculinity quotient is always high, guaranteeing steady business and steadier sex. Just don't be surprised by the somber stares when you push back the black curtain to enter the bar—especially if you're wearing jeans. Dress to impress.

Also held at Argos, "Amster-den" is the bi-monthly weekend for bears and their cubs. Check the website for further information.

CASA MARIA, Warmoesstraat 60, Tel. +31 (0)20 627 68 48, www.casamaria.nl. A cozy bar in the sense that two dozen customers might prove a fire hazard, this is a superb place to window watch, especially if you enjoy watching stoned tourists, drunk Brits and other glaring stereotypes unwittingly stumble through Amsterdam's leather stretch. Casa Maria is compact, draws a mixed, unpretentious crowd—everything from tattoo-and-piercing-laden leathermen to their older sisters—and like many of the city's gay bars, claims to be one of its oldest. Its best features by far are the huge windows facing the Warmoesstraat, prime real estate in Bizarreoland.

COCKRING, Warmoesstraat 96, www.clubcockring. com. Highly popular and filled to capacity on the weekends, the Cockring is a leatherish bar/dance club that lives up to its reputation—be it leather, early 20s, Spanish tourist, or Viagra-inspired. A three-level club with an upstairs bar, the venue is a one-stop shop for shamelessness, where punters can watch live masturbation shows onstage, hit the furnacelike

LEATHER LUST

DON'T FLOG yourself for missing Amsterdam's last Leather Pride. The October event is a must for kinky leathermen and rubber slaves looking for a sordid rendezvous. For information on tickets, or other leather/fetish events happening throughout Holland, check out www.leatherpride.nl.

darkrooms, dance their little tank tops off, or drink themselves under the bar, though not necessarily in that order. Small by major metropolis standards (the city doesn't boast Berlin-size industrial warehouses) the Cockring is easy to navigate, and has everything to offer because anything and anyone goes here— possibly because there are no other choices. Because there's no strict dress code, the clientele ranges from brawny leather studs eager for a rub down to boys who buy their beauty at the tanning salon.

THE CUCKOO'S NEST, Nieuwezijds Kolk 6, Tel: +31 (0)20 627 17 52, www.cuckoosnest.nl. Popular for hours that begin early enough for commuters to have a ride before catching the train home, the bar itself is nothing special. But its true claim to fame is a subterranean darkroom, supposedly Europe's largest, filled with red-lit cabins, glory holes, and dark crevices. The bar tends to draw a sleazy and mixed crowd so when it comes to action it's really hit or miss. But on winning days, you'll hit the jackpot.

DIRTY DICKS, Warmoesstraat 86, Tel: +31 (0)20 627 86 34. Sleaze at its best, Dirty Dicks is true to its name. A late-night weekend leather bar that occupies the Eagle's former hunting grounds, it's sometimes crowded, other times not. Upon entry, the bar appears disappointingly empty but once your eyes adjust to the shadows, you'll see a constant flow of patrons emerging from the back caverns.

EAGLE, Warmoesstraat 90, Tel: +31 (0)20 627 86 34. Located within several strides of the Cockring, the Eagle looks like a typical Amsterdam bar—old. Extremely crowded during the weekends, the three-level bar attracts an approachable, diverse crowd but the bar itself is easy to miss unless you find the doorbell and ring it. The first floor has a pool table with a sling, and downstairs the cellar is a large cruising area with several cabins. Patrons tend to flit back and forth between the Argos across the street like attention deficit sex slaves, as the Eagle gets busier closer to closing time.

The Eagle also hosts the occasional rubber-only parties sponsored by Black Body.

Not on Warmoesstraat but Definitely Leather

DE SPIJKER, Kerkstraat 4, Tel: +31 (0)20 620 59 19, www. spijkerbar.nl. The Spijker is certainly less rawhide than it used to be, but this friendly neighborhood leather bar still has some edge—mainly, a busy pool table and vintage porn videos. An odd but nice

CLUE

DARKROOM ETIQUETTE

When entering bars with darkrooms, the unwritten rule is: always buy a drink first. If you don't, you will be chased down and publicly humiliated—which will hurt your chances of getting laid. Though most boys love a rebel, here it's just considered cheap.

touch, the management plays porn and cartoons side-by-side, appealing to boys of all ages, and possibly triggering latent memories of junior high jack-off sessions. The sublevel bar pulls a diverse crowd, but is particularly popular with those in their 30s–40s, and also women. Upstairs you'll find one of the smallest darkrooms in town, but there are usually more balls in action at the pool table, or watching the barmen pour drinks. On Tuesdays, there's an all-day beer bust, and on Saturdays, there's bingo. Happy hours: 5–7 p.m.

THE WEB, St Jacobsstraat 6, Tel: +31 (0)20 623 67 58. A cruisy, well-established leather bar around the corner from the Cuckoo's Nest, the Web also operates early. Beyond its corrugated iron façade, the interior is dark with winding stairs leading up to a large, mazelike darkroom that's not too dark. With requisite porn videos, raunchy atmosphere,

NATURAL BEAR HABITAT

CLUE

Nope, no full-on bear bars here, but bears are known to ramble through Café de Barderij, the Web, and Argos. For bear events, your best bet is the Dikke Maatjes website (www.dikkemaatjes.nl), which includes events like the Bear Sauna (at Thermos Day Sauna, first Saturday of the month), the occasional Bear Hug parties. Want bowling? There's a bear night in neighboring Utrecht.

and a dildo lottery every Wednesday night, the Web manages to spin its own flavor of rough intrigue.

A Place of Our Own

THANKS TO colonialism, the Netherlands has an increasingly diverse population. But this is far from reflected in bars—gay or straight—for Moroccan, Turkish, Asian, Mediterranean, Caribbean, and Surinamese communities. Here are a couple:

HABIBI ANA, Lange Leidesedwarsstraat, 4-6, www. habibiana.nl. Arabic for "my sweetheart," Habibi Ana is Amsterdam's only Arab gay bar and claims to be the only one in the world. An oasis for a melting pot of Turkish, Moroccan, and Egyptian gays, the bar's steamier than a Turkish bath but mostly from too much tobacco smoke, hookahs aside. More like a lounge with garden benches, rattan stools, and comfortable couches, the bar is frequented by effeminate Arab boys and older, potential sugar daddies. The music, of course, is Middle Eastern, met with occasional belly dancing by a mixed crowd (in age, sex, and race). Amsterdam has a large Muslim immigrant population but religious attitudes have often kept many closeted, making the bar, which continues to do business despite an undercurrent of homophobia (within its own community), a surprise hit.

REALITY, Reguliersdwarsstraat 129, Tel: +31 (0)20 639 30 12, www.realitybar.nl. Reality is as tropical as it gets in wintry Amsterdam. Catering to men from the former colonies—Surinam, Indonesia, and the Netherlands Antilles—the bar boasts a Caribbean carnival vibe year-round and a largely black clientele that likes to get their meringue on. The bar, which is located closer to Rembrandtplein, is small, smoky, and bustles with a regular crowd. Here, window shopping costs but the price of a drink.

A POSTER FOR "CLUB TRASH" TRASHING REMBRANDT.
COME AND PLAY.

CHAPTER 7

Dance, Dance, Dance

Sex and disco,
the ultimate mix.

IF YOU expect to be energized by disco drama, the hypnotic sway of fabulously overendowed go-go boys and gay mega-club glamour, Amsterdam, which earned its party reputation over a decade ago, doesn't live up to its former hype. While the publicity was always skewed, the scene suffered a severe blow in 1999 when fire gutted the legendary, absurdly creative RoXY. Soon after, in-house drug arrests sealed the outrageous iT's fate, leaving thousands of gay boys all dressed up with nowhere to go. Much of the scene eventually packed up, migrated to a warmer reception elsewhere or packed it in all together, leaving Amsterdam looking like Priscilla, Queen of the Deserted.

But that's not to say the scene is completely dead. To be fair, Amsterdam is small and the dance scene has always reflected this—and what major capital actually boasts packed gay clubs on a Monday night? Scratch beneath the surface, and there's still a lot going on in unexpected locations, monthly parties, and increasingly at straight clubs that are seeking to queerify in order to diversify. Amsterdam is certainly no London, but if you spend the weekend you'll discover a scene busy reinventing itself, especially at alternative parties, which are old-school Amsterdam and decidedly less commercial.

Rather than harp on the negatives of recently departed clubs or club nights, this guide seeks to accentuate the positives. While the Cockring is the only gay club open 7 days a week, the Exit on Reguliersdwarsstraat is popular weekends, as well as You II (listed in chapter 6). Sundays, the young and the restless visit squat club Trut—more of a watering hole than disco—and the rest of the week, most gays flit between mixed venues, alternative parties, and gay nights.

The following is a list of gay or gay-friendly dance clubs followed by regular weekly and monthly gay nights and finally special events, like those organized around Gay Pride.

Regular Outings/Venues

COCKRING, Warmoesstraat 96, www.clubcockring. com. The city's most popular gay club (due to nil competition), the Cockring's unofficial motto is: "Sex and disco, the ultimate mix." Far from the super-gay Eurovision sing-a-longs you'll find at other bars, the Cockring boasts renovated cabins, naked parties and live pornographic performances on stage every Thursday. At the club, all kinds of muscular beefcake sponsored by the liquor industry scamper between floors, flirting, dancing, and entering the darkroom that's as hot as a kiln. Despite its location along the leather belt, the club's not strictly leather so anything goes—especially because everyone goes here.

In addition to its normal activities, the club holds the Nude Club every first Sunday, a nude sex party where shoes and enthusiasm are the only things that make it past the entrance. Doors open 3–4 pm Also, look out for Asian Disco Night every third Sunday of the month, with fantastic drag shows, free snacks, a bevy of Asian boys and their dedicated admirers.

ESCAPE, Rembrandtplein 11, Tel: + 31 (0)20 622 11 11, www.escape.nl. By far one of Amsterdam's largest venues, the Escape has been around since 1987. If you don't mind long lines and gratifying the doorbitch to chance one of its revolving nights, the club offers standard nightclub fare: exclusive parties; a young, chic clientele; a multitude of atmospheric lights; multi-media backdrop; pricey drinks; and at times, strangely arrogant attitude. That said, the ever-popular gay Salvation party—sadly re-imported to the U.K. in 2006—was held regularly here, attracting its fair share of enthusiastic studs and the club's celebrated "Chemistry" nights on Saturdays also changed venue to warehouse-sized club Marcanti (see listing for JoyRide XL parties on p. 146). Still a progressive club venue, the Escape offers something for everyone as well as Escape deluxe, its posh club within a club, which hosts a number of gay events.

STRAIGHT OLD DAMES— AMSTERDAM STAPLES

MELKWEG, LIJNBAANSGRACHT 234, Tel: +31 (0)20 531 81 81, www.melkweg.nl. Located in a former milk factory, the Melkweg offers live music during the week and dance music at the weekend. There are also media events, theater, and exhibitions, and daily performances by local, unknown, and big name acts. There's no dress code, no door policy, and no hassle. Not gay, it offers diverse entertainment.

PARADISO, Weteringschans 6-8, Tel: +31 (0)20 626 45 21, www.paradiso.nl. Like the Melkweg, the Paradiso is mostly a live music venue but also hosts club nights with top international DJs, festivals, and special events. Housed in a former church initially squatted by hippies, it's famed for being a premiere music venue and cultural stage that boasts high ceilings, a balcony overlooking the centramainl dance floor, and an international lineup of acts. Pink Floyd, Rufus Wainwright, and thousands of bands in between have played here over the decades, as the Paradiso averages 700 acts a year. Often the first local venue where underground DJs play, it hosts several annual gay events such as the Love Dance.

EXIT, Reguliersdwarsstraat 42, Tel: +31 (0)20 625 87 88. Once a staple on the gay scene, the Exit has scaled back its opening hours but still attracts young weekend crowds and its fair share of Thai kathoeys (lady boys), who happily thump to a variety of music styles (with four dance floors, there are four choices). Considered trendy by giggling gays and in need of a severe makeover by others, it's really the only other gay dance venue outside the Cockring, which guarantees a largely male audience when and if it's busy. Like many gay venues, it's not crowded until late, sometimes not until neighboring Soho closes its doors, and its third-floor darkroom is often an afterthought.

JIMMY WOO, Korte Leidsedwarsstraat 18, Tel: +31 (0)20 626 31 50, www.jimmywoo.com. The sleek side of local clubbing, Jimmy Woo's boasts a spectacular dance floor lit by 12,000 bulbs where the well-connected boogie Hong Kong Triad–style. There are huge lanterns, Hirake art, dark sofas, an opium table, and the downstairs dance floor can easily fit 400. Swanky in its best and worst sense, the club draws local celebrities, poseurs, and people-watchers, who usually have good reason to look, but the crowd is predominantly straight. Dress like you've got class or just fake it and you might be able to squeeze past the door Nazi. Inside, there's a mix of R&B, hiphop, disco, and soul. Gay-friendly; Wednesdays are gay nights.

OCCII, Amstelveenseweg 134, Tel: +31 (0)20 671 77 78, www.occii.org. With a name that sounds like an obscure tax document, the OCCII is a former squat that specializes in alternative/experimental,

SQUATS

AMSTERDAM HAS a relatively large squatter community, though nothing compared to the '80s when a housing crisis pushed the issue to the forefront. Squatting is simply occupying an abandoned or unoccupied space in order to reclaimitsuse—eitherforlivingorsocialactivities. During the '80s, large, deserted warehouses and residences were squatted by groups of students and activists and became breeding places for alternative culture, as well as bars and theaters. Many have been closed in recent years, though a few remain today. Amsterdam's institutions like Paradiso and Melkweg were once squats, as well as the fashionable hemelse modder restaurant (see p. 97).

underground/hardcore, and non-commercial music. Often noisy and sporting a crowd almost young enough to fit the Harry Potter demographic, the venue specializes in freaky, groovy, or just plain weird bands that tout their obscure sounds in equally unintelligible wordage—like "nauseating death-rattle dirge." The décor is pure Dad's garage/ storage shed but it's the crowd that exhibits all the color. This is a mixed venue where everything goes, and club-goers take the words "Express Yourself" (even Madonna's version) literally.

Spellbound Productions, a queer collective,

frequently hosts parties such as Blackbox and Disco Hospital at OCCII.

PANAMA, Oostelijke Handelskade 4, Tel: +31 (0)20 311 86 86, www.panama.nl. This upscale restaurant/nightclub/theater is located on the city's edge in the trendy Zeeburg warehouse district. Relatively new and large by local standards, the two-level club is sleek, with a solid sound system that has drawn DJs such as Howells, Deepdish, Digweed, and Tiesto, big-name Cuban bands, and a largely older, moneyed crowd. Not a gay club, occasional gay mega events such as the women-only Flirtation are held here. If you're willing to make the trek and don't mind the straight hordes, Panama is a highly commercial (read: stylish but soulless) alternative to smaller city clubs.

RAIN, Rembrandtplein 44, Tel: +31 (0)20 626 70 78, www.rain-amsterdam.com. It's raining techno, hallelujah. A hip hybrid club/bar/restaurant on touristy Rembrandtplein, Rain is terribly stylish, but the atmosphere is mostly sterile and the prices terribly steep. Make it past the bouncers, and the interior is visually impressive, the sound system good quality, but the dance floor is small and the clientele mostly older/straight. While the seasonal Sunday Rain Tea Party (held the first Sunday of the month from November to April) here is rather well attended and cruisy, Rain is typical trendy tourist fare.

STUDIO 80, Rembrandtplein 17, Tel: +31 (0)20 521 83 33, www.studio-80.nl. A new venue for electronic dance music, Studio 80 mixes DJs, performances ,and music styles, offering everything from techno club sounds to live bands, with an emphasis on showcasing up-and-coming talent. Multifunctional, bringing together music producers and festival organizers, the studio is also a venue for a variety of gay nights, such as Fashion Radio (www.radio-activity.nl), a monthly party with resident DJ Lupe that features the talents of stylists and fashionistas. There's also Blackbox, a monthly night held by ArtLaunch (see next page), presenting local and international talent with techno, minimal house, acid, and electro music. And finally, Multisexi, a new, open-minded gay party.

SUGAR FACTORY, Korte Leidsedwarsstraat 12, Tel: +31 (0)20 627 99 92, www.sugarfactory.nl. The Sugar Factory opened its doors in 2005 and despite its small size, has exercised large-scale, creative ambition. Coining itself a "night theater," the venue, which sits just opposite the Melkweg, offers a dizzying array of dance nights, cabaret, DJs, and live performances, including fashion shows, art, and raw, experimental stage acts—no surprise, considering it was established by members of the renowned, eccentric Winston Hotel. Drawing a mixed crowd (in age, race, and sexual orientation) that likes to dress up as much as they get down, one of the venue's best features has to be closing its doors at 5 a.m. Pity they don't serve breakfast here…yet. The Sugar Factory regularly runs gay events, such as the weekly Vreemd.

SUPPERCLUB, Jonge Roelensteeg 21, Tel: +31 (0)20 344 64 00, www.supperclub.com. Mention leisure suits, fleece sweaters, or Barry Manilow here and you're likely to be kicked to the canal. A trendy restaurant/lounge/performance art space, Supperclub serves dinner and entertainment first, but guests are expected to dance for their dessert. Overtaken in recent years by straight tourists and pretentious Eurotrash, it's still stylish enough for gay tourists to be entertained—at least by the waiters.

Weekly or Semi-Regular Dance Nights

ARTLAUNCH, various venues, www.Artlaunch.nl. WEEKLY. Somewhat alternative dance/performance art/fashion parties, ArtLaunch embarked in 2002 with a bang but has since rapidly accelerated towards bust. Once a combination of innovative acts, visuals and underground DJs, the parties expanded from Amsterdam to Berlin, Barcelona, Istanbul, and São Paolo but became less edgy and weathered with age—an unfortunate truism for most things in the physical universe—and were scaled down considerably. Thursdays, ArtLaunch café is held at the Queen's Head, featuring DJs from Amsterdam and Berlin, and makes for a good pub night out, though nothing of its former glory.

ASIAN DISCO NIGHT, held at the Cockring, Warmoesstraat 96, www.clubcockring.com. MONTHLY. Held every third Sunday of the month, with fantastic drag shows, free snacks, and a bevy of Asian boys and their dedicated admirers. Women welcome and the €5 entry is reasonable.

CLUB CUT, held at the Sugar Factory, Korte Leidsedwarsstraat 12, www.clubcut.com. EVERY FEW MONTHS. Transforming movie titles into theme nights, Club Cut—a Dutch spin on words, *kut* means, er, "vagina" and is often used as an expletive—is a tacky party full of terrific entertainment. A recent effort by local gay boys, including a KLM flight attendant, who decided to take matters into their own adept hands, the parties follow themes such as "Best Little Whorehouse in Texas," and "One Night in Paris." Musically, you'll trip through the decades, arriving at feel-good house. Entertainment can be shocking and meant to stir debate.

CREW LOUNGE, held at Escape Deluxe, Amstel 70, www.crewloungeevents.com. EVERY FEW MONTHS. Created by KLM (Royal Dutch Airways) queers near the cockpit (that's flight attendants) tired of being taken for a ride when it came to their nights off, Crew Lounge is a hip party catering for those in business class. Held the first Sunday of every third month at different venues, the sold-out party offers house DJs and entertainment and sends proceeds to children in developing countries, allowing party goers to be fashionable with a cause. Tickets are conveniently available at the airport Crew Center or online.

DANSERETTE, held at Akhnaton Nieuwezijdskolk 25-27, www.Danserette.nl. EVERY FEW MONTHS. Danserette, relatively new on the scene, boasts an über-Dutch atmosphere with disco lights, glitter balls, and healthy doses of Eurovision hits, disco classics, and music that falls into the category "Après Ski." Held the first Sunday of the month at Akhnaton, a café/hall/society established by Catholic students to focus on world music, the party is well attended though the fliers tend to look more fashionable than the folk—predictable given Dutch fashion standards.

DISCO HOSPITA, held at OCCII Amstelveenseweg 134, www.spellbound-amsterdam.nl. EVERY FEW MONTHS. An underground party held by queer collective Spellbound Productions, Disco Hospital follows on the tails of the collective's renowned Planet parties (which had a decade-long run) and sticks to a similar format. Music runs the gamut from techno and minimal house to dub, and the offbeat crowd (featuring types that like to wear vomit-colored army boots, or asymmetric Mohawks) is equally varied. Definitely no Muscle Marys here—they'd be far too queer for this funky, androgynous crowd.

Spellbound used to run Flush It parties, where underground DJs spun in the urinals, and toilet paper and water sports were a must. Look out for future Spellbound parties, some of the most innovative on the Amsterdam scene.

FLIRTATION, held at Panama, Oostelijke Handelskade 4, Tel. +31 (0)20 311 86 86, www.letsbeopen.nl. EVERY FEW MONTHS. Packed to its rafters with estrogen, Flirtation at Club Panama proves that lesbians know exactly how girls like to have fun. While the women-only event is held six times per year, it draws more than 1,000 women each time, transforming the club into a smoky den with divas turning on their heels to requisite house music, flirting, and hooking up. The event, incredibly successful and big enough to give all-male gay events a run for door numbers, has had several themes running from Mardi Gras to

Latin Salsa, though the crowd wears whatever it feels like—from femme to androgynous. The music tends to run cheesy house, proving that both sides of the gay spectrum need their ears cleaned.

FRESH, held at the Sugar Factory, Korte Leidsedwarsstraat 12, www.clubrapido.com. BI-MONTHLY. A bi-monthly party provided by Rapido, Fresh brings the beach party atmosphere to Amsterdam. To be expected: pectoral beefcake twisting to energetic, progressive house; barely-clad boys; a sea of dilated pupils; endowed go-go boys who definitely get fresh; theatrics; glam attitude; flirtation; and enough sweat to swab the floors. The same goes for Rapido's larger bi- to tri-annual party, held at the renowned Paradiso and which boasts top-notch international DJs, including Madonna producer Giagi Cappey, massive crowds, and the energy to easily compete with parties in Barcelona or Berlin.

HI VICTORY, held at Queenshead, Zeedijk 20, www.hivictory.com. BIMONTHLY. Hi-five to this party, a bi-monthly event for people with HIV and AIDS, which celebrates the living and those who support them. Held at the Queen's Head, it features surprise acts and music from DJ Jarb.

STETSONS, held at Zuiderzeeweg, Tel: +31 (0)20 436 12 73, www.stetsons.nl. WEEKLY. Flaunting queer country cool and proud of it, the cowboys and cowgirls at Stetsons like to kick it until the Dutch-belted cattle come home. Amsterdam's first and only country western dance club, Stetsons evolved out of line dance lessons and has been going strong since 1993. On Mondays, there are beginner classes and

Tuesdays are for advanced students who know how to wrangle in their Wranglers. Occasionally there are larger Gay Western Saloon bashes where you might spot your very own Marlborough Man.

VREEMD, held at the Sugar Factory, Korte Leidsedwarsstraat 12, www.gajealvreemd.nl. WEEKLY. Held at an intimate venue, Vreemd, which means "strange," boasts DJs, VJs, and performers who skirt the line between avant-garde and tongue-in-cheek.

An extension of Vreemd, and a monthly event, Wildvreemd, won a Gouden Kabouter or Golden Gnome award for best new night initiative and one of the best steps they've taken is free entry, guaranteeing cheap gays (you know who you are) more pocket money for their boozing habits.

Also, Pink Blink hosts a Pride Women's party and pre-Christmas gig for lesbians with Vreemd. Check out the Sugar Factory's website for more details if you happen to be in town.

DE TRUT, Bilderdijkstraat 165, www.trutfonds.nl. WEEKLY. Make the drinks cheap and they will come. Around since 1985 but still one of Amsterdam's best kept secrets, de Trut is a queer disco/bar housed in a former squat. Cool, non-commercial, relaxed, and incredibly mixed, the nonprofit seized upon a winning formula—cheap entrance (€1.50), cheap drinks, strict gay/lesbian door policy, limited capacity, and a laissez-faire attitude—and hasn't looked back since. Staffed by volunteers, the bar has an underground, unorthodox appeal and draws a chatty crowd in their twenties who dress however they feel. Because DJs play for free, the music varies widely, but that's part of its rough-edged charm, although they've had to turn the volume down due to the neighbors. Open Sundays from 11 p.m. to 4 am, it's best to line up well before opening time, or you might not get in—there's only space for 200. The later and drunker it gets, the more the atmosphere takes off and you can always say you staggered home for a good cause—because de Trut recycles its profits back into the gay community.

UNK, held at Club 8, Admiraal de Ruijterweg 56, Tel: +31 (0)20 685 17 03, www.club-8.nl. MONTHLY. A mixed underground club night held at Club 8 every last Saturday of the month, UNK takes a no-nonsense approach—it's all about the music. Organized by DJs who wanted to get back to basics, mainly electronica in its heyday, UNK helped put Club 8, a pool hall/restaurant with a graffiti-covered hall upstairs, on the map. While organizers are apt to add descriptive letters to the front to beef up interest (like P, F, H or SP—yeah, spUNK), the party is always popular and there's a relaxed atmosphere. The regular crowd is young 20-somethings who, unlike most of their friends, prefer venturing out in the physical world to online Internet chat. On other nights, Club 8 goes Xanadu and hosts roller disco, though the music is hip-hop.

VRANKRIJK, Spuistraat 216, www.vrankrijk.org. WEEKLY. Countering the pessimism at the start of the work week, Blue Mondays offers live music for gays, lesbians, and those who are on the fence and want to check out the competition. Held at the legalized Vrankrijk squat, a stalwart of Amsterdam's fading squat scene and run by volunteers, the drinks are accordingly cheap, the entrance free, and those who go there tend to fall in the left-wing/neo-punk/old-school anarchist category, even if they were born way later. The squat holds a queer party every last Monday of the month, as well as alternative parties every Saturday.

Circuit Parties

CO2 SENSATIONS, held at Powerzone, Spaklerweg, Tel: +31 (0)20 681 88 66, www.co2party.com. Touting itself a "polysexual party experience" for trendy people, this mega party held at the spacious Powerzone doesn't believe in false advertising. A combination of gorgeous bodies, international DJs, pumping global house music, and wild lighting topped off with CO^2 cannons straight from Ibiza (that shoot cold carbon dioxide into the steamy crowd), Sensations continues to grow. Shuttle buses leave every 15 minutes to the venue, located just on the city's southern outskirts—a ride worth taking if you're looking to work up a good sweat.

JOYSTICK, held at Marcanti Kingdom, Jan van Galenstraat 6-10, Tel: +31 (0)20 320 50 56, www.joystick-amsterdam.com. A German party that migrated north in 2004, Joystick is all lights (hundreds of 'em), camera (strike the pose, boyz), and action (energetic dance orgy!). Held five times a year at the gigantic Marcanti Kingdom, a large rented venue in the west of Amsterdam, the party boasts a sea of sweaty, shirtless men, seductive transvestites, theatrics, muscular mayhem, and Ibiza-inspired euphoria.

A musical playground for hedonists with fabulous acoustics, Joystick is a typical gay circuit party and one of Amsterdam's finest.

A spin-off of Joystick, **JOYRIDE XL** is a 14-hour non-stop clubbing extravaganza with local and international DJs, playroom areas, punters going ga-ga for go-go, and hours of exposure. Also held at Marcanti Kindgom (www.kingdomvenue.com), better known as Kingdom and with a 1,500 capacity, the party is a collaboration between well-known event organizers GROUP NL (Joystick Amsterdam, Sleaze Ball) and Riedijk Productions (White Party, CO_2 Sensations).

JUICE, held at Hotel Arena, 's-Gravesandestraat 51, www.juice-amsterdam.com. A good place to party with your main squeeze, Juice is one of Amsterdam's most recent gay events, held at former church Hotel Arena. Still getting its feet wet, the party has yet to pack the house (which holds up to 1,100) but the music is sexy, and the sound system, solid. The party stops at 4 a.m., earlier than most, but you can still catch a tram back to your hotel— or try for a party with a longer history and hours.

LOVE DANCE, held at Paradiso, Weteringschans 6-8, Tel: +31 (0)20 626 45 21, www.paradiso.nl. A creative, collaborative effort by a running list of local gay organizations, the Love Dance was launched as an annual HIV/AIDS awareness party and an outgrowth of Worlds AIDS Day. Held since 2003 at the well-loved Paradiso, the benefit offers live music, onstage performances, fashion, DJs, and a beautiful, mixed crowd that come together to celebrate life, not just survival. All artists work for free so proceeds go straight to the fight against AIDS. The event's main aim is to promote awareness and safe sex, and help curb a disease that currently kills 353 people each hour.

ORANGE BALL, different venues, www.reidijkproductions. com. One of the queer community's annual Queen's Day parties, the Orange Ball (the color of Holland's royal family) is definitely orange, but the event itself has become increasingly gray. Organized by Riedijk Productions, which has received growing flack over the years for dragging its clogs and offering over-hyped parties, the event, which started in 2001 and sells out year after year, usually draws a huge cache of hot men dancing, drinking, and waiting for something more exciting to happen—musically at least. Oh, you pretty things, don't you know that you're driving the organizers insane?

SLEAZE BALL, held at Marcanti Kingdom, Jan van Galenstraat 6-10, Tel: +31 (0)20 320 50 56, www. sleazeball.nl. Relatively new to the scene (which changes as quickly as a tranny's wigs during a full cabaret performance), this party is for those into leather, rubber, PVC, or sporting an Adidas addiction. Created by Erick Verhagen, who also helps organize Joystick, the ball is sweaty, sleazy, with xxx shows, play zones, and a big dance area for full pelvis contact.

WHITE PARTY, different venues, www.reidijkproductions. com. For those who like their whites ultra bright, the White Party, also organized by Riedijk Productions, is super-clean fun. Low on sex drive but high on

SAFE-SEX PARTIES

WHEN IT comes to combating AIDS, GALA (Gay and Lesbian Amsterdam) has been vigilant. A non-profit association that organizes (safe) "Sex on Sundays" (SOS) at the Eagle bar, GALA has put immense energy into keeping the message alive. "HIV and STD rates are up year after year in the Netherlands," says Elard Diekman, GALA's acting head, "and Amsterdam is the epicenter."

GALA began holding monthly SOS parties at Argos in 1998, but after several years of proven raunchy popularity, the parties were increased to twice a month. "Give the boys what they want," jokes Diekman, noting that while most events are full, there's still a need to actually enforce the rules. "When we see someone having unprotected sex, they are asked to leave—which unfortunately, happens regularly," he says. "We don't really like to police but without condoms, there's no justification for having these parties."

While SOS provides unlimited free condoms, Diekman laments that most local venues have a habit of only handing out one. "That's good old-fashioned Dutch stinginess," he says, adding that he believes the city should swamp gay bars with condoms.

joy, the party offers happy house music and puts the crowd in high spirits—possibly because everyone looks like they've just arrived in heaven. Quite a successful party for its blissful vibe.

Men-Only Parties

Weekly

For those who don't like to pay for sex (unless you count breakfast the next morning), Amsterdam offers several venues where sex is free. Well, really the cost of a beer. Or three.

JACK OFF PARTIES, held at Stablemaster, Warmoesstraat 23, www.stablemaster.nl. Home to almost nightly Jack Off parties hosted by ex-stripper Tony Starr, the Stablemaster attracts older exhibitionists ready to unzip at the door but not necessarily eager to go to home base. The bar is small, and the parties can be hit or miss, depending on who shows up. But anything generally goes—except for bare feet.

SAMEPLACE, Nassaukade 120, Tel: +31 (0)20 475 19 81, www.sameplace.nl. If anywhere in Amsterdam can be tagged a sleazy vice den, this is it. Open for anybody and everybody, including swingers, shemales, fetishists, exhibitionists, and really, Amsterdam's most seedy, the bar serves those who want to be serviced or drool over a pint while watching live demonstrations. Mondays are men-only nights, with a one item dress code, and the action is usually hot. But if you want a really *dark* darkroom, you'll need to look elsewhere.

RENT BOYS

AMSTERDAM IS famous for its Red Light District, but when it comes to gay boys renting out their bodies, there are no neon-tainted windows to be found. Instead, they tend to loiter around Paardenstraat off Rembrandtplein, which in its heyday drew closeted men looking for lust, or today on Internet sites. In 2004, Why Not Bar, one of the city's largest boys clubs, went bust, leaving the city with one true gay bordello: the Music Box. Otherwise, those looking for working boys have well-advertised cyber options.

THE MUSIC BOX, Pardenstraat 10, Tel: +31 (0)20 620 41 10. Amsterdam's last surviving hustler bar, the Music Box draws mixed reviews—mostly warning customers to watch their wallets. Many of the Eastern Europeans who work here are gay for pay (as with many escort services) and cash poor, so keep your head on straight because they ain't called hustlers for nothing.

MICHAEL'S BOYS ESCORTS, www.michaelsboys-escorts.com. This is a gay-owned business offering the services of men between 18 and 35 years old. Escorts make hotel or private apartment visits and cost €140/hr.

PEOPLE, www.peoplemale.com. Started by two university students who were obviously do-ing their homework, People offers a selection of boys ranging from 18 to 35. Good reputation, regularly updated website. Rates start at €145/hr.

More websites to try for escorts

Click on the English flag for descriptions/information in English (for those who never studied geography, history, or just never studied, it's red, white, and blue, with a huge X through it).

www.boys4u.nl
www.boy4male.com
www.bestboys.nl
www.chatboy.nl

SEX ON SUNDAYS (SOS), held at the Eagle, Warmoesstraat 90, Tel: +31 (0)20 627 86 34. For non-churchgoers who like to pray at a different altar, SOS doesn't disappoint. Often packed to capacity, the party gets started right at the door where half the men immediately undress, though most wait a few gulps into a beer before making a move towards the darkroom. Chatty, with friendly attitude, guests tend to pace themselves but once the action starts, it can be hot, horny, and wild, with sex happening all over the bar, against it, and a slew of other appropriate prepositions. Organized by the nonprofit GALA (Gay and Lesbian Amsterdam), which endorses safe sex and provides unlimited condoms and lube, the party sticks to strict guidelines—no safe sex and you're out.

Monthly

HORSEMEN AND KNIGHTS, held at the Cockring, www. ncadam.com. Every third Sunday of the month, Horsemen and Knights gather in search of the ultimate Excalibur, putting their sizeable sheaths on display. Held at the Cockring, the party welcomes 100 or so naked/semi-naked participants with hefty blades, though average-sized peasants are also welcome. Safe sex is the norm. Condoms and lube are free and readily available. For those who've worked up an appetite so big they could eat a horse, sandwiches are served afterwards. Entrance is €7.50, enter at 3–4 p.m., ends at 7 p.m.

NUDE CLUB AMSTERDAM, also at the Cockring, www. ncadam.com. Held the first Sunday of the month (leaving Amsterdam with only one sex-free Sunday, what to do?), this event is for naked, excitable, horny men eager to reenact their fantasies of attending a Viagra convention. Safe sex only, and promising loads of action, these popular parties live up to the maxim "anything goes." Entrance is €7.50, enter at 3–4 p.m., party ends at 7 p.m.

More infrequent

BLACK BODY AND EAGLE RUBBER ONLY PARTIES, War-moestraat 90, www.blackbody.nl. Held three times a year, this exclusively rubber party is an all out Gum-mi fest for serious aficionados. Check on the website for dates.

GIRLZNSTYLE, held at Club Latido, Buikslotermeerplein 7/9, www.girlz-n-style.com. A more intimate, newer version of Flirtation. A women-only party held at

Club Latido, the crowd only reaches about 200. Club, Latin, and tribal tunes. This has just got off the ground, so we hope it keeps running!

PERVERTS, held at Exit, Regulierstwarsstraat 42, www.clubperverts.com. Much hyped but still not widely (or wildly) attended, this imported Berlin party injects kink into the otherwise vanilla Exit venue. Strict leather/rubber dress code and safe sex only.

XXXLEATHER, www.xxxleather.nl. A party that evolved from in-fighting at the COC, XXX is a well-run, highly organized nonprofit fetish fest high on imagination and low on cost. Held at the spacious Lexion, a 45-minute drive out of town, the venue is transformed into a kinky dream palace with a sizeable dance floor, two playrooms, and Tantric leather pursuits in every artistically light crevice. XXX grew quickly, from 500 to 1,200 men within several parties, thanks to international DJs, local VJ talent, artists, masseurs, volunteer inspiration, and the ultimate drive to party for fun, not for profit. Four free shuttle buses, which include onboard entertainment, ferry participants across town so once you arrive, you're straight on the dance floor, no lines necessary. Safe sex only, and condoms and lube provided for free.

XXX also holds monthly get-togethers at the Spijker bar, last Sunday of the month, and women are also welcome.

OUT IN THE OPEN

WHEN IT comes to the historical side of cruising, Matthias Duyves knows his urinals. "There were two hundred at the end of the 19th century but they were all removed after World War II, when the space was exploited for parking," says Duyves, a secretary of Dutch Parliament who has written extensively about gay use of public space. "And since the '80s, darkrooms have pushed cruising indoors."

But Amsterdam's parks are still active, though cruising issues have changed—sometimes in odd ways. Take Nieuwe Meer, a remote stretch of land just south of the city and frequently cruised by gays, which eventually became an important ecological site. To protect the land, the local council introduced Scottish Highlanders and fenced much of the area off, perhaps a covert call to halt gay wildlife. "But the cows are actually extremely friendly," says Duyves. "The first one I saw immediately turned its bottom to me. It was as if they were trained!"

Annual Dance Events

PLAYGROUNDS, www.leatherpride.nl. A large fetish party held during Leather Pride, Playgrounds is like stuffing San Francisco's Folsom Street Fair into a nightclub, ditching the Porta-Potties in favor of shower rooms and shouting "1-2-3-ORGY!" Strict leather and rubber only, the party is like a perverse game of Twister, only nobody loses once their feet leave the ground. Special shuttle bus services to the—*shhh!*—secret location are provided. Safe sex only and save the attitude—that's what your outfit is for.

WASTELAND, www.wasteland.nl. A famous, mega, mixed fetish party, Wasteland is for rubber cross-dressers, pansexuals of any ilk, glam exhibitionists, Goths, aspiring medical practitioners, gays, bi's, and possibly anything plummeting back from the future that managed to make it past a metal detector. Tagged "probably the wildest party on earth," by *Penthouse* magazine, the party is a surreal voyage into the sexual fantasies of thousands of participants and exotic enough to knock the socks—or latex leggings—off even the most seasoned of pervs. There are three dance areas, gay and straight performances, and a fully-equipped dungeon. Every corner is a lush wasteland of spontaneous, kinky seduction.

Cruising: You Better Shop Around

WHEREVER THERE'S a patch of green in Amsterdam, guaranteed there's gay men cruising it. The quick sex, no-strings-attached appeal of public, late-night sex still holds its charms, though virtual hookups have proven stiff competition in recent years. So where to do it? We're suggesting a mere handful of better-known or frequented places, but the key to any mutual groping is: be discreet. While locals can be relatively tolerant, local councils, responsible for condom cleanups, are not. If you're caught, you can be fined €100. Also, when police patrol at night, it's usually to ensure public safety, not harass gays—which looks bad on their records—but they will shine a light when you're misbehaving. While there are no official opening hours, cruising tends to happen late-night.

NIEUWE MEER, OR DE OEVERLANDEN A large expanse of land found halfway towards Schiphol airport, this area—a far stretch for those without a car—is an active cruising spot for provincial out-of-towners, locals with transport and ambitious cyclists. Facing a beautiful lake (or "*meer*"), the area boasts bike paths, flush foliage, ample trees to lean against and, thanks to the local council, dopey Scottish long-horned cattle initially meant as a cruising deterrent but which soon proved absolute bull. Getting there is somewhat of a challenge, but you can take the subway to the Henk Sneevlietweg stop, walk westwards to Johan Huizingalaan (and the IBM building), take a left, and walk towards the Mexx building, then walk under the overpass until you reach the parking area. Then you can start spotting prey.

OOSTERPARK, take trams 3, 7, and 9. This park is in a working-class, immigrant neighborhood with a large representation of Turk, Moroccan, Caribbean, and Surinamese immigrants. Busier over the summer months, the action happens on the eastern corner near the skating ring and bridge. Some of the men here may be closeted due to cultural or religious norms, so it's best to stay alert when you emerge into a neighborhood that has some of the same issues.

SARPHATIPARK in de Pijp area. Named after Samuel

Sarphati, a Jewish doctor who helped create a city garbage removal service (shame it doesn't apply to his namesake, which has a reputation for discarded condoms), this attractive, active park in the funky de Pijp neighborhood draws action near the basketball courts on its southeast corner. A busy children's park by day, it's often policed by night, so be discreet and remember to take your worn prophylactics with you—or little little Johnnie (or *Jaap* in Dutch) might find it the next morning and proudly show his mama.

VONDELPARK off the Overtoom, south of the city. A favorite of Amsterdammers, this extensive park attracts picnickers, footballers, cyclists, dogs, and just about everyone in the city longing for fresh air—meaning it's a great pickup place for gays and straights alike. About midway through the park, the Rose Garden attracts a fair share of pretty boys, but the action is at night, earlier than other cruising areas around town. The park lies in an upscale neighborhood, but you'll find ambitious locals occasionally trying to fleece the unsuspecting, so be savvy.

THE PINK POINT, THE ONLY KNOWN GAY KIOSK THIS SIDE OF
THE ATLANTIC.

CHAPTER 8

Resources Directory

Waar zijn de kroegen?
(Where are the bars?)

FOR ALL those other practicalities, such as annual events, media resources, how to get your mouth around some Dutch (language, that is), chase free legal advice, zero-in on gossip, or broaden your working knowledge of the city, here's a run down on the whats and wheres you'll need to further your adventure.

Annual Gay Events

DARKROOMS AND discos aside, some of the best reasons for gays to visit Amsterdam are annual events that bring the LGBT community together to celebrate its diversity and oh, some Dutch stuff, too. So here's a list by calendar date:

ROZE WESTER FESTIVAL, April 29. Held the night before Queen's Day at the Homomonument, the festival kicks festivities off with the Drag Queen Olympics, including a handbag toss—dangerous when those divas, trying to avoid breaking any nails, fling bulky secondhand shoulder bags into the audience. Partying continues on Queen's Day, when the whole city goes ape.

KONINGINNEDAG (QUEEN'S DAY), April 30. The Dutch, who are born mercantilists, found the perfect way of marking their Queen's birthday—by turning the city into an all-day, open-air flea market, selling used junk, and wearing orange, the royal family's color, to excess. If you didn't know the Dutch had a real Queen—Beatrix (who resembles a friendlier Thatcher) —they do, only they celebrate on her mother Juliana's birthday, April 30, when the weather supposedly warms up.

During the day, you'll find children performing on musical instruments for money (gotta train 'em young), outdoor concerts, boats filled to capacity with orange partiers, bobbing along the canals like over-sized Cheetos, people buying, others selling, lots of drinking, smoking, and outrageous spontaneity in every quarter as the city's population doubles and crams in for the event. The party gets started the night before on Koninginnenacht (don't try saying this if you're chewing gum), and continues through to the day itself.

Gay parties are held along the Amstel, in the Reguliersdwarsstraat and at the Homomonument, and look for venues advertising for the night before. If you want to see how the Dutch do carnival, this is a must-see and one of the most enjoyable events of the year.

AIDS MEMORIAL DAY, May. International AIDS Memorial Day remembers the victims of AIDS. Held at the Dominicus church, the event includes speeches, songs sung in remembrance of those who have died, as well as quilts displaying their names. The ceremony is concluded with a rendition of Bette Midler's "The Rose," followed by the release of hundreds of white balloons.

NATIONAL REMEMBRANCE DAY, May 4. The COC's Amsterdam branch holds a two-minute silence at the Homomonument, followed by speeches and a wreath-laying ceremony (in Dutch).

LIBERATION DAY, May 5. An all-day queer event, with performances and an outdoor party also held at the Homomonument.

AMSTERDAM LITERARY FESTIVAL, end of May, www.amsterdamliteraryfestival.com. A bold attempt by local journalist Pip Farquharson via BritLit (which she co-founded) to put Amsterdam on the literary map, this new festival features lesbian, queer-friendly, and underground authors, proving that gay festivals (this is not technically gay, but the organizer is) can be held off the dance floor. Past award-winning speakers include Jeanette Winterson (*Oranges Are Not the Only Fruit*), Sarah Waters (*Fingersmith)*, Valerie Mason-John/Queenie *(Borrowed Body)*, and Judith Weingarten (*The Chronicle of Zenobia*). The festival just hit its second-year mark, but promises to continue strong, bringing fresh impetus to both the local and international writer's scene.

AMSTERDAM PRIDE, August, first weekend. One of Europe's largest gay and lesbian festivals and the local

WILD SIDE, www.wildside.dds.nl. A local woman's S&M group that takes play seriously, Wild Side meets regularly at the COC offering forums and discussions for novices and veterans alike. Sincere about pushing technique, engaging in genitorture, and discussing everything from blood sports and flogging to writing erotic fiction, the group takes a highly professional approach (in Dutch and English) to the delightfully dark world of S&M. Here, learn the ropes and you'll be tied to them.

gay community's most anticipated event, Amsterdam Pride is an extended weekend of street parties, parades, gay-themed exhibitions, sports competitions, and film festivals. All gay for a three-day run, the festival offers so many different events it's enough to frustrate true party queens who strive to be in two places at once (or today, try 20). One definite highlight is the Saturday afternoon Canal Parade—the world's only gay floating pride—with roughly 80 colorful boats watched by thousands of onlookers (guestimates put it at 350,000) working hard for the next day's hangover. With parties before, after, and during the event, there's little chance of staying completely sober and if it rains, who cares because it's absolutely overflowing with possibilities.

HARTJESDAG, August, third weekend. Just when you thought drinking beer and cross-dressing weren't for breakfast anymore, the Dutch celebrate Hartjesdag

(Day of Hearts), an annual festival dating back to the Middle Ages, with ample doses of both. While the festival's origins aren't exactly clear, it's thought to stem from a day when locals were allowed to hunt deer in the forests around Haarlem and later barbecue their catch on Amsterdam's streets. During World War II, Nazis halted celebrations but in 1997, local businesses revived the event, which is celebrated now along Zeedijk. For those wanting to experience streets crowded with towering cross-dressers parading to generic Dutch pop, this festival's for you.

WALP (WOMEN AT AMSTERDAM LEATHER PRIDE), Sept/ Oct., www.walp.dds.nl. A conference for aspiring Cat Women, WALP packs a wallop for international leatherwomen wanting to dig their heels in. The small conference, founded in 1996 and bi-annual on even years, has scaled back from ten lengthy discussion days to four with more punch. Events include a slave auction, workshops, and the unexpected degradation of the final party if no one actually asks you to dance.

TRANSGENDER FILM FESTIVAL, www.transgenderfilmfes-tival.com, November. Previously held in Amsterdam and Rotterdam, this celluloid fest celebrates gender diversity by featuring five days of premieres, panel discussions, lectures, spoken word performances, sneak previews, documentaries, and experimental shorts. Time/venue to be announced. Keep up-to-date via their website.

LEATHER PRIDE, November, first weekend. A joint venture created by Amsterdam's leather daddies (Black Body, Rob, Leather, and Mister B), Leather

Pride is Europe's largest leather-rubber-fetish happening, though still smaller than its North American counterparts. Several thousand men—from the hyper-masculine to bratty sluts—gather for four days of skin festivities, including flashing their fishnet tanks, strutting in studded pouches, and pleading for public humiliation. There are dozens of parties, exhibitions, sex shows, and the like to loosen inhibitions, up the voltage, and push participants to the sextreme.

ROZE FILMDAGEN, December, second or third week, www.rozefilmdagen.nl. An international film festival showcasing a potpourri of queer talent, the event airs experimental films, videos, and discussions with queer filmmakers. Venue announced on website.

The Local News

IF YOU'VE GOT some time to kill between cups of coffee and want a good read, look out for the following publications:

AMSTERDAM WEEKLY, www.amsterdamweekly.nl. An English-language paper aimed at local Amsterdammers, tourists, and resident expats, the *Weekly* covers local arts/entertainment and general listings, and consistently examines gay themes. Free, the publication is distributed throughout the city and can be found at the American Book Center.

BUTT, www.buttmagazine.com. A pocket-sized, pink-paged "fagazine" that's honest about fucking, fetishes, and fashion, *Butt* keeps its content 100 percent real.

AMSTERDAM WEEKLY

IT'S NOT easy to set up a free, award-winning cultural newspaper, but that's exactly what Todd Savage did in 2003. Savage, a freelance journalist with the *Chicago Reader*, had relocated earlier to Amsterdam after an assignment covering several gay European capitals for Frommer's unexpectedly led to love. "I finally moved here because it was easier," he says referring to Dutch immigration laws that recognize same-sex couples. "At home it would have been much more difficult to 'import' my partner."

Savage eventually spotted a niche and *Amsterdam Weekly* was born. To date, it has been a successful venture. The independent paper grabbed three European Newspaper Awards and is distributed at 600 locations around the city.

Of Amsterdam, Savage says his first impressions ("everyone is *very* tall") haven't changed significantly over the years. "The one thing that struck me was how open and uninhibited gay people were talking about going to saunas, kinky parties, or darkrooms. There was really no stigma attached, whereas I think gay Americans would be more prudish," he says. Yet paradoxically, Savage finds America's gay community more on-the-edge. "Because gay people are fully emancipated in Holland, being gay seems more matter-of-fact," he says. "In America, it's more ghettoized and has more of a political aspect to it."

As for Amsterdam's status as a gay Mecca, Savage believes it has changed, as all things do over time. "Amsterdam had a certain moment when it was a legendary city for its extravagant parties—that's gone. But tourists are fickle and always want to be in the next buzz city, like Barcelona." Yet in terms of tolerance, he says, little has changed. "If you're a gay kid and this is your first time to Amsterdam, it's Nirvana."

The magazine is an intelligent, voyeuristic trip that's crude, graphic, sordid, witty, and has captured the imagination of a growing international audience. Published locally in English, you can find it at Vrolijk.

GAY NEWS, www.gay-news.com. This is a widely distributed, bilingual monthly publication targeting news, shopping, and travel issues and featuring in-depth reports covering a wide gay spectrum in the Benelux region. The website has just surpassed 1.7 billion hits per year and hard copies are available in bookshops and selected venues.

GAY & NIGHT, www.gay-night.nl. A monthly lifestyle magazine with event listings, there are some English articles, though the majority are in Dutch. Also available at bookstores or free two weeks after publication in selected gay venues.

GIRLS LIKE US (GLU), www.glumagazine.com. Created by Jessica Gysel, who once produced *Kutt*, *Butt* magazine's sister issue, GLU is meant to blur

CLUE

The Amsterdam Gay Map is published once a year, with a 100,000 circulation, and is distributed at gay venues throughout the city. Dutch Royal Airlines KLM also produces its own corporate edition.

boundaries, sustain subversiveness, and bring a playful, fresh perspective to lesbian subculture. Young and brash, it offers a mature exploration into rebellious lesbian chic. Published locally in English, it's available at Vrolijk.

Internet Resources

FOR INTERNET aficionados, these are good resources for extensive gay listings (in English):

DAN & ROLLO'S NIGHT TOURS, www.nighttours.nl. Take a virtual tour of the city on this website, which evolved out of two previously successful sites covering gay goings-on. Listings include a complete party agenda, pictures, gossip, reviews, and input from local boyz. For those interested in taking day trips, the site also provides listings for Rotterdam, Utrecht, Brussels, and Antwerp.

GAY AMSTERDAM, www.gayamsterdam.com. The Gay News' online site for listings and classifieds, it offers extensive hotel and restaurant listings, reviews, and an interactive gay map perfect for helping you get your bearings. Mostly in English, accompanied by impossible-to-pronounce Dutch street names.

For a full listing of all local gay websites, try www.gayamsterdamlinks.com in Dutch and English, or for an extensive party agenda or tickets, try www.gaygo.nl.

I AMSTERDAM, www.iamsterdam.com. The city of Amsterdam's most recent marketing initiative and cheesy motto to garner greater attention, I Amsterdam is the city's official English website. Here you'll find city-specific news, tourist information, business networking, research and statistics, gay and lesbian information, and recommendations by local writers—some queer, others not—deemed "I ambassadors." An excellent resource for general tourist information.

UNDERWATER AMSTERDAM, www.underwateramster-dam.com. Set up by Pip Farquharson, a freelance British journalist who moved to Amsterdam in 1992 and never looked back, this site includes listings of what's currently on, a film agenda, unusual hangouts, queer information, and a comprehensive section for lesbians. The ever-curious Farquharson, who also founded BritLit, the Amsterdam Literary Festival, a website for Amsterdam DJs (she DJs, too) and edits GLU magazine amongst other journalistic exploits, has got her active fingers in many pies, and her site, which is constantly updated, reflects her extensive interests.

YAGO TRAVEL, Holton, Tel: +31 (0)54 837 76 18, www.yagotravel.nl. This travel agency is an initiative by the

HOMOMONUMENT

CONSIDERING AMSTERDAM'S collection of phalluses—such as Amsterdammertjes or the enormous National Memorial on Dam Square—most tourists expect the Homomonument to sport a similar erection and inevitably walk past it. But designed by a woman, local artist Karin Daan, the monument is much more subtle. Consisting of three equilateral triangles made of pink granite that together form a fourth, larger triangle, the Homomonument addresses both men and women while symbolically articulating gay history.

The idea to create a monument for the thousands of gays persecuted by Hitler's regime circulated immediately after the war. But it wasn't until the 1970s, when gay and lesbian emancipation movements were in full swing, activists pushed for gay inclusion in memorial services—decades after the National Memorial commemorating Dutch soldiers and resistance fighters had been built. In 1979, the government finally granted its approval, but it would take another decade for gay organizations to raise the money to complete it.

The triangle, of course, was the sign issued by the Nazis to brand gays and later adapted by the gay community to embody its emancipation. At the Homomonument, three triangles represent past, present, and future. Set in the ground and pointing to the Anne Frank House, the triangle signifying the past bears the words of gay poet Jacob Israel de Hann, "Such an unlimited longing for friendship." Anne Frank was also deported by the Nazis and this is a warning against history repeating itself. The present is characterized by a triangle extending over the Keizersgracht canal, pointing towards the National Memorial. This is where people come to lay flowers and remember all gays who have been, or continue to be, persecuted. A third triangle raised above the ground doubles as a podium and meeting place and points towards the COC, the world's oldest gay and lesbian organization. This represents the future, as a place for gays to express themselves as they continue to fight for visibility.

Every year, people gather at the Homomonument on May 4th, national Remembrance Day, to commemorate gays and lesbians who lost their lives during WWII, as well as honor those who continue today to struggle for freedom. On May 5th, Liberation Day, local queer groups gather at the monument again to party and celebrate its vision—to be grounded in the present with an eye to the future, but never forgetting the past.

Gay Krant and offers occasional Happy Hour tours through Amsterdam, as well as publishing its own *Travel Tour* magazine, full of gay travel stories, ideas, and tips. While the agency is located in Holton, you can call for more information on its international and European travel destinations.

LGBT Resources

CENTRE FOR CULTURE AND LEISURE (COC), Rozenstraat 14, Tel: +31 (0)20 626 30 87, www.cocamsterdam. nl. Amsterdam's branch of the national gay and lesbian emancipation organization, the COC is a meeting place that sponsors gay initatives to advance gay integration within Dutch society. A popular center for gay events, discussions, and dance nights since its inception during the 1940s, the Amsterdam headquarters suffered acute cash flow problems in 2006 and subsequently shut down its social arm, which it claimed was unprofitable. The city of Amsterdam saved the local offices from bankruptcy, but its future survival is still in some doubt as the organization continues to be restructured. Their website contains limited English information on free legal advice, education programs, and workshops.

GALA (GAY AND LESBIAN AMSTERDAM), Tel: +31 (0)20 676 23 17, www.gala-amsterdam.nl. A volunteer-run venture, GALA organizes festivals at the Homomonument, safe-sex parties at the Eagle bar, and hold parties on Queen's Day and during Amsterdam Pride. The boys here also like to gussy up in drag, so look out for the Drag Queen Olympics the night before Queen's Day.

GAY & LESBIAN SWITCHBOARD, Tel: +31 (0)20 623 65 65, www.switchboard.nl. The Switchboard is a good first source for information on everything from drugs

PINK POINT

OPENLY GAY in Amsterdam's bustling tourist center, Pink Point gay information kiosk is one-of-a-kind. Located next to Homomonument, Pink Point came into being for the 1998 Gay Games but its popularity demanded an encore. The kiosk, which morphed from a temporarily converted ice cream cart to its current guise, offers free advice year-round. Says Pink Point founder Richard Keldoulis, the kiosk is more than a gay tourist hub—mostly, because it's just meters away from the Anne Frank House. "The question we get asked most is 'Where's the Anne Frank House?' Only one day, someone asked 'Who's Anne Frank?'" he says, laughing. Luckily, question number two is how to find the Homomonument. "That's really why Pink Point exists—to give the monument, which represents the serious side of gay life, higher visibility," says Keldoulis.

If high visibility helps create greater acceptance, Pink Point is doing its job—not just for the monument, but for Amsterdam's gay community. In addition to providing information on the Homomonument and Amsterdam gay and lesbian life, the kiosk flogs queer-themed souvenirs, T-shirts, postcards, gadgets, and queer Delft blue figurines to boot. "Because we don't sell porn, people feel safe coming in. We've become a kind of public forum," says Keldoulis, noting how many tourists and locals stop by to discuss homosexuality or talk about relatives who have come out. "We're often someone's first contact with the gay community."

Keldoulis loves his job, especially because it allows him to drive home how special Amsterdam, his adopted city, is. (An Aussie transplant, he met and later married his Dutch partner here). "We're a real capital," he says, likening Amsterdam to Washington, D.C. "We might not have the glam and glitter of London, Paris or Berlin, but we have a hugely diverse, concentrated gay community with a lot of political depth," he says. "We've put a lot of effort into coming together to improve our lives."

and dating to coming out and is available seven days a week (M–F 12 pm to 10 pm, Sat/Sun 4 pm to 8 pm) by phone or Internet on an anonymous basis. The service has operated since 1986 and English-speaking volunteers are extremely supportive. The Website provides links to gay venues throughout the Netherlands.

HIV FOUNDATION (VERENIGING), Eerste Helmersstraat 17, Tel: +31 (0)20 689 25 77, www.hivenet.org. A checkpoint that offers anonymous HIV testing with results within 15 minutes, the organization also provides information on healthcare, medication, alternative remedies, and leaflets. Information is available on their website or over the phone in English, Spanish, French, and Portuguese.

INTERNATIONAL HOMO/LESBIAN INFORMATION CENTER AND ARCHIVES, Nieuwpoortkade 2A, Tel: +31(0)20 606 07 12, www.ihlia.nl. Also known as Homodok, this GLBTQ archive/library/information center carries over 4,100 periodicals dating back to the dawn of the gay emancipation movement to contemporary queerzines, coming-out guides, handbooks for gay and lesbian parents, and an extensive collection of information ranging from local politics, legislation, and popular culture to music and entertainment. IHLIA's Amsterdam branch (there's another in Leeuwarden) is a bit out of town, but the website provides excellent directions on how to find its small office. The friendly staff is helpful answering requests and helping you find the information you need.

PINK POINT OF PRESENCE, on Westermarkt, Tel: +31 (0)20 428 10 70, www.pinkpoint.org. Just south of the Homomonument, this gay information kiosk/souvenir shop offers free advice, information on the latest gay and lesbian parties and events, as well as gay publications and souvenirs. Volunteer run, PPP funnels profits into the monument's maintenance as well as gay happenings that highlight GLBT visibility.

Wat zeg je? (What did you say)? Language Tips

FOR THOSE who have never studied another language and rely on English, there's little to worry about when you arrive in the Netherlands. The Dutch are linguistically gifted and it's safe to assume most Amsterdammers (that's 99.9 percent) speak English, in addition to German, Spanish, Italian, French, Russian, Thai, Hindi, and probably Esperanto. That said, a few well-placed words or phrases are always appreciated by the locals, so we'll list them here. But good luck, the pronunciation is a *verdomd lastige toestand* (a bitch).

Q FACT: According to *Newsweek*, the average Dutch teenager speaks English better than his or her American counterpart.

Common Phrases

hallo: hello
dag/doeg: goodbye
altstublieft/alsjeblieft: please (formal/informal)
dank u/je wel: thank you (formal)
bedankt: thank you (informal)
ja/nee: yes/no
Ik begrijp het: I understand
Ik begrijp het niet: I don't understand
waar zijn de…clubs/gay clubs/restauranten/kroegen?: where are the… clubs/gay clubs/restaurants/pubs?

For reading film schedules or other events, you'll see ma. (*maandag*/monday), di. (*dinsdag*/tuesday), wo. (*woensdag*/wednesday), do. (*donderdag*/thursday), vr. (*vrijdag*/friday), za. (*zaterdag*/saturday), or zo. (*zondag*/sunday).

1–10: *een, twee, drie, vier, vijf, zes, zeven, acht, negen, tien.*

Food

ontbijt: breakfast
lunch: lunch
avondeten/eten: dinner
dagschotel: dish of the day
eetcafe: café (that serves food)
kip: chicken
varkenvlees: pork
rundvlees: beef
bitterballen: fried beef/mincemeat croquette
broodje/boterham: sandwich
soep: soup
salade: salad
nagerecht: dessert
koffie: coffee
thee: tea
water: water
sinassappelsap: orange juice
wijn: wine
bier: beer

Shopping

winkel: shop
kassa: check-out counter
ik wil graag.....kopen: I'd like to buy…
waar is/ zijn....: where is/are
apotheek: pharmacy/chemists
spoor: platform (at train station)
strippenkaart: tram/metro ticket
kaartje: train ticket
fiets: bicycle
politie: police

In terms of lingo, it goes without saying the Dutch are a direct people—if they weren't, the country would be flooded—leaving their language far removed from romance. Calling someone an ass or a little shit is actually a term of endearment and insults run more along the lines of *"Je bent uit de baarmoeder gerukte boskabouter"* (you're a forest gnome ripped out of the womb). Far too advanced for tourists. But here are some more colorful terms:

trut: bitch

flikker/nicht: a queer

sexy/prikkelend: sexy

klootzak: son of a bitch (literally, testicles)

kut: vagina/pussy (used as an interjection like shit, e.g., *"kut weer,"* or shitty weather)

hoerig/sletterig: whorish/slutty

kontneuken: anal sex

lul: cock/dumb person

pijpen: to give a blow job

schatje: babe

stout: naughty

Afterword:
Something to
Take Away

QUOTE

Make pilgrimage—this is a
gay Mecca, after all.

AMSTERDAM, an ancient city with a modern reputation
built on liberal attitudes, fierce independence, and
warm hospitality remains one of the most gay-friendly
cities on the planet. A popular destination for gay and
lesbian tourists from around the world, the city became
a center for the international gay liberation movement
and has since retained an aura of tolerance. While the
city's reputation as a legendary paradise where the
social laws of gravity simply don't apply has always
been an impossible ideal to live up to (and something
locals would never readily boast), Amsterdammers
take their "live and let live" attitude seriously. Here,
anything goes because anyone—from gays and the
politically persecuted to Euro hippies—is welcome.

Amsterdam today remains a fascinating experiment

in progress. It's a place where gay life has become an integral part of the city's very texture—so much so that many local gays see gay-only establishments as almost passé. Still, there are plentiful gay venues, nightspots, hotels, and shops scattered throughout and gay festivities thrive the hotter it gets. But that's not the only reason to visit. Unlike larger, crowded cities that resemble concrete canyons, Amsterdam is peaceful and compact. Every few blocks there are shops offering fresh bread or delicious cheese, beautiful canals lined with cafés, cobblestone streets, endless bike paths, and a diverse population that hails from every corner of the globe. And at night, despite its major capital status, it's quiet—unless you're meandering through the Red Light District or cruising deep within the Warmoesstraat's darkrooms. The city offers incredible choice—enough to keep restless night owls, sexually charged customers, casual dope smokers, early-risers, or run-of-the-mill tourists fully occupied.

But don't take our word for it. Visit. Make the pilgrimage—this is a gay Mecca, after all. Discover Amsterdam's devotion to social tolerance, take the message home and declare it loudly. The Dutch are seasoned traders, thrilled by exchange, and this one idea they are more than happy to export.

Notes

p. 18   In the first year alone: Kees Waaldijk, "Latest News about Same Sex Law," Universiteit Leiden Meijers Institute, http://athena. leidenuniv.nl/rechten/meijers/index. php3?m=10&c=76, last viewed June 14, 2006.

p. 18   Lesbian couples: Gay News, interview with Central Bureau of Statistics, vol. 176, April 2006.

p. 18   The first signs: Amsterdam Historical Museum "Goed Verkeerd" Exhibition (10/89-2/90) school notes for classroom instruction, IHLIA Homodok Lesbian Archive.

p. 19   Amsterdam's first guidebook: Jo Durden-Smith, Departures,www.departures.com/tr/tr_0100_amsterdam.html, June 8, 2006.

p. 19   Dutch poet: Ludy Giebels, "On de Haan," Cyber Corpse Issues 5 and 6, http://www.corpse.org/issue_5/critical_urgencies/giebels.htm, last viewed June 8, 2006.

p. 20   In 1904: Gert Hekma, Encyclopedia of Homosexuality, www2.fmg.uva.nl/gl/eoh.html, last date of access June 8, 2006

p. 21   Its passage: Theo Sandfort, "Boys on Their Contacts with Men," Elmhurst, NY: Global Academic Publishers (1987).

p. 23   Bar culture: Gert Hekma, The Amsterdam Bar Culture and Changing Gay/Lesbian Identities, written for University of Amsterdam's Gay and Lesbian Studies, www2.fmg.uva.nl/gl, June 8, 2006.

p. 23   In its first years: Johan Roest, Johan's World of Beautiful Men, http://home.tiscali.nl/cb002147/gay_life.html, last viewed June 8, 2006.

p. 23   No longer queers: Ibid

p. 25   Radical faggots: Amsterdam Historical Museum "Goed Verkeerd" Exhibition (10/89-

2/90) school notes for classroom instruction,
IHLIA Homodok Lesbian Archive

p. 25   As early as 1632: Amsterdam Historical
Museum "Goed Verkeerd" Exhibition (10/89-
2/90) school notes for classroom instruction,
IHLIA Homodok Lesbian Archive.

p. 25   In 1792: Ibid

p. 27   Fortuya, who was anti-immigration: Richard
Goldstein, "Fighting the Gay Right," *The
Nation*, July 1, 2002

p. 28   A case in point: Expatica, Expatica News In
Brief April 12, 2006, http://www.expatica.
com/source/site_article.asp?subchannel_
id=19&story_id=29254&name=Dutch+new
s+in+brief%2C+12+April+2006, last viewed
June 8, 2006

p. 35   Average High Temperature: Gate1 Travel,
Netherlands Average Temperatures, http://
www.gate1travel.com/europe-travel/weather/
Netherlands-weather.htm, last viewed June 8,
2006.

p. 36   While taxis: Stephen Pemberton and Astrid
Kerssens, "The Internet Guide to Amsterdam,"
http://homepages.cwi.nl/~steven/amsterdam.
html, last viewed June 14, 2006.

p. 44   80,000 bicycles: Royal Institute of Navigation,
"Dutch Track Bicycle Thieves with GPS,"
March 2004, http://www.rin.org.uk/pooled/
articles/BF_NEWSART/view.asp?Q=BF_
NEWSART_93417, last viewed June 14, 2006.

p. 45   Its population: Dara Colwell, "Riding to the
Rescue," *Village Voice,* August 29, 2005.

p. 45   Marijuana status: Netherlands Ministry
           of Foreign Affairs, "Q&A Drugs 2003: A
           Guideline to Dutch Policy," http://www.
           minbuza.nl/default.asp?CMS_TCP=tcpAsset
           &id=175A6D3F70164607A386D43B61DC13
           5FX2X42819X14, last viewed June 8, 2006.

p. 45   As a result: Netherlands Ministry of Health,
           "Welfare and Sport, Drugs Policy in the
           Netherlands," http://www.ukcia.org/research/
           dutch.htm, last viewed June 8, 2006.

p. 45   As for weed: US Department of Health and
           Human Services (HHS), Substance Abuse
           and Mental Health Services Administration,
           National Household Survey on Drug Abuse:
           Volume 1. Summary of National Findings
           (Washington D.C.: HHS, August 2002), p.
           109, Table H.1 (listed on www.drugwarfacts.
           org/thenethe.htm).

p. 48   1,498,205 inhabitants: Amsterdam Tourist
           Convention Board, Facts & Figures, http://
           www.amsterdamtourist.nl/en/home/
           about+amsterdam/facts+_xan_+figures.aspx,
           last viewed June 8, 2006.

p. TK   Straat means street: Iamsterdam, "Canals,"
           http://www.iamsterdam.com/introducing/
           nature_geography/amsterdam_water/canals,
           last viewed June 14, 2006.

p. 85   Washington's own diary: www.erowid.org/
           plants/cannabis/cannabis_history2.shtml

p. 118   From thinkexist.com, http://en.thinkexist.
           com/quotation/the_thrifty_maxim_of_the_
           wary_dutch-is_to_save/164750.html, last

viewed June 14, 2006.

pg. 147　The even'ts main aim: Clubvan2000, "Wereld AIDS dag," http://www.clubvan2000.nl/index.php?page=10_4_1&articleId=244, last viewed June 14, 2006.

pg. 156　Getting there: http://groups.msn.com/nieuwemeer/_homepage.msnw?pgmarket=nl-nl

Acknowledgments

I would like to thank all of those who made this book possible—those I interviewed, the Pink Point of Presence, the bartenders, sales clerks, restaurant staff, and customers who informed me along the way; Gert Hekma at the University of Amsterdam for his expansive historical expertise; the incredibly helpful, informed staff at Homodok; and, of course, Amsterdam for its beautiful, beautiful self.

About the Author

DARA COLWELL has written extensively about gay lifestyle and social issues since penning her first article on AIDS as a high school reporter. A former investigative journalist at *San Jose Metro*, her numerous articles appear in publications such as the *Village Voice, Details,* and *Penthouse.* While earning her master's degree from UC Berkeley's Graduate School of Journalism, Dara interned with *Frontiers* magazine. Later freelance pieces included "Rainbow Journalism" (*SF Metropolitan*), "Gay with God," *(Alternet.org)*, and "Boys on Film" *(Bust* magazine). Dara now lives in Amsterdam, legendary adult playground and liberal Mecca, where alternative culture is considered the norm—just how she likes it.